MEE
DIV(

"One of my relatives who is happily married, said to me, 'Look out for whom you meet. Look at us, we dated from our freshman year!' And I thought, That's the kind of life I'd like to have. But I answered, 'Oh, no, I'm not going to college to meet somebody. I'm going to study.' Yet in the registration line the next day when I met this attractive young man who wanted to be a professor, I thought our relationship had been preordained, really a blessing. For the next four years, I dated no one else."

Nina Hibbert

"Divorce is like standing in the middle of a burning house, where the only exit is through a burning door. If you go through it, you know you will be scarred. But the alternative is to stay and die."

Sara McDevitt

"It's tempting to look for a man to take care of me, but I enjoy the feeling of making my own decisions and having my own money. And if I do remarry, I'll never go back to scratch where I have nothing in my own right. Even if I win millions of dollars in the lottery, I'll keep working."

Alice Crouch

DIVORCED WOMEN, NEW LIVES

Ellie Wymard, Ph.D.

BALLANTINE BOOKS • NEW YORK

Library of Congress Catalog Card Number: 89-92437

ISBN 0-345-36322-1

Manufactured in the United States of America

First Edition: May 1990

For Buddy

ACKNOWLEDGMENTS

I am grateful for

the trust of forty-five women who must remain anonymous; but without their words this book would not have been written.

friends who believed in this project, and recommended women for me to interview.

the generous professional advice of Barbara H. Behrend, CFP; Rev. Ralph P. Brooks, Ph.D.; Jane Coleman; Eileen Colianni, M.S. Ed., N.C.C.; Mary Devlin, Ph.D.; Peggy L. Farber, Esq.; Dr. Herbert I. Levit; Nancy Mac Leod; Patricia Miller, Esq.; Partricia G. Milligan, CFP; Rose Palmer-Phelps; Ellin Wymard, Esq.; Joseph M. Wymard, Esq.; the research of Denise Overfield; and the spontaneous day-to-day concern of my colleagues, Edith Benzinger and Jane Gerety.

the loyalty, intelligence, and sensitivity of Mary Ann Eckels, my editor.

two loving sons, Josh and Peter, who frequently watched over my shoulder as words appeared on the computer screen—my first readers; the friendliest of critics.

the irrepressible enthusiasm and boundless love of Buddy, my husband.

TABLE OF CONTENTS

Introduction

This book is the result of interviews with women willing to share details of their marriages and divorces so that women in similar situations might benefit from their experiences. Their stories prove that it is possible for divorced women to start new lives after having lived through domestic turmoil, heartache, and grief. The women who speak throughout this book maintain that it is within the power of a divorced woman to act upon her future by recognizing that she has choices to make. She can choose not to be a victim of divorce, no matter what she has suffered.

Divorced women arrive at the point of accepting responsibility for their self-definition in various ways. But crucial to all of them is a willingness not to short-circuit natural feelings of anger and disappointment, as these emotions can motivate them to change the condition of their lives. Women who are unhappy in their marriages will often repress their anger by claiming, instead, of feeling "old," "tired," or "depressed." Until they admit their anger, they cannot use it constructively or even cure their false symptoms. On the other hand, a woman who perpetuates anger and disappointment can thwart her development toward self-knowledge and self-esteem. If hostility prevents her from honestly analyzing why she married the man she did, and why their marriage ended in divorce, she risks repeating the behavior that helped to create such sad results. By holding on to anger, she becomes, at best, a breathing memorial to the wrong that was done to her. The choice is clear: get even or get well.

At the time of their divorces, the women interviewed for this book did not have charmed solutions for their problems. Some of them confide that it was hard to dress in the mornings, even to leave their beds. A young woman now tells us, laughing, "My thoughts were so crazy that I once hard-boiled seven eggs and then thought, Now I won't have to cook for the rest of the week." But these women have done more than survive. Each one tells a different story of attaining personal success, fulfillment, and happiness. Yet common to all of them is a willingness to be introspective, face who they are, and accept where they have been. Even the humor of their situations does not escape them. They set goals and act to achieve them. Truly, they are proud of their accomplishments. They appreciate life as a fleeting moment in time, which, as one woman says, "can't be put on hold." Some draw strength from a reservoir of values that they acknowledge as a legacy from their parents. Others must learn to reject their parents' values as a harmful heritage. Many rely on prayer as a source of grace. But guiding them all is a commitment to urge other divorced women to explore their talents and opportunities with vigor so that their futures are indeed their own to decide. For this reason only, they have told their stories. Hence the book, *Divorced Women, New Lives*.

CHAPTER 1

Triumph, Not Survival

The Grace Kelly syndrome was so strong that when I went into labor with my first child, I had to take time to remove four hundred pins from my French twist.

Elizabeth Hampsey
June 4, 1987

But Elizabeth Hampsey, age fifty, is now one of a growing number of divorced women, once ornamental accessories to their husbands, who has attained financial independence by developing a professional career or starting a business.

Elizabeth left an abusive, alcoholic, entrepreneurial husband to achieve her own status as a successful attorney with a New York law firm. Her journey from paddle tennis court to corporate boardroom involved three poverty-stricken years isolated with her children in a modest apartment while she attended law school.

Granted a divorce settlement of only three thousand dollars, without alimony because of her husband's declared bankruptcy, Elizabeth depended upon student loans and minimum-wage jobs to complete her law degree in 1980 at age forty. She also lived on welfare and arranged for her children to benefit from a free lunch program at their elementary school. She sold her clothes, fur coat, and jewelry but claims that she missed nothing about her previous life except a "year-round suntan." Elizabeth insists, "There was no way that law school was not going to work. I had to achieve something of my own in order to protect my kids. But to remind myself that things would not stay this way, I took out a subscription to *Architectural Digest*."

Divorced Women, New Lives is about women like Elizabeth Hampsey who are propelled by the crisis of divorce to change the course of their lives. These women, from various socioeconomic backgrounds, speak in their own voices about their successful struggles to achieve independence. Their first experiences of personal triumph often involve mastering a skill that they had previously abdicated to their husbands: pitching a tent for the children's annual camping vacation; driving a car for the first time on a crowded freeway in order to register for a financial planning course in the city; bicycling forty miles with two young daughters, without husband blazing the way on his Schwinn. But these homey images of newfound confidence do not remain static. They culminate with these same women succeeding as corporate executives, starting businesses from scratch, or taking themselves seriously as writers and artists.

For this book, forty-five divorced women, who are proud of their accomplishments, tell the stories of their marriages so that women in the cycle of divorce will gain heart that it is possible to start again. Without crowning themselves as heroines, they want other ordinary women to be sustained and strengthened by their example. Even though the recovery from divorce is never a straight line, they believe that a divorced woman has a chance to find comfort, insight, and the power to act when she recognizes her own experiences in the life of another.

Despite the popular images of chattering women spilling their secrets at quilting bees and coffee klatches, women have been private about revealing their deepest thoughts. Only with the spread of consciousness-raising groups in the seventies did women begin to talk freely with each other about the details of their daily lives, uncovering patterns in the experiences they shared. Women felt validated when hearing their unspoken thoughts and feelings articulated in many different voices. Traditionally, women confided intimate concerns to their private diaries, long safeguarded from public eye on the basis of their triviality. Even when expressed in imaginative literature, the inner lives of women have been invisible because the works of women writers were slow to enjoy wide publication and serious consideration in school curricula. But divorced women will often rely on novels when wanting to learn from women whose problems resemble their own.

The morning after her husband left their home, a young woman recalls rushing to her local bookstore to buy a copy of *Madame Bovary*: "I devoured it trying to find clues about myself and why my marriage had failed. I really needed to feel some affinity with another woman, so I turned to fiction. Madame Bovary was the only woman character who came easily to my mind, but

I really wanted to read about someone closer to my own time and place."

From fiction, women expect to move into the reality of their own lives, searching for solutions. But long accustomed to reading about uniquely feminine experiences from the perspective of male writers, they now enjoy the option of finding emotional and psychological identification with a variety of women characters in novels written by women.

For example, when reading the classic American novel of World War I, *A Farewell to Arms*, no one can agree that Hemingway's understanding of Catherine Barkley is realistic when her primary concern, during childbirth, is to please her lover, Frederick Henry, and the doctor.

On the other hand, critics in 1899 suppressed *The Awakening*, a novel by New Orleans writer Kate Chopin, for describing a young mother's growing dissatisfaction with her marriage and her feelings of sexual awakening with a younger man. Moreover, Chopin's frank observations on childbirth also offended critics, especially when the heroine, Edna Pontellier, helps a friend during labor: "With an inward agony, with a flaming, outspoken revolt against the ways of Nature, she witnessed the scene torture."

The Awakening, written at the turn of the century in New Orleans and not reprinted in the United States until the 1960s, is now standard reading in American literature classes. This fact in itself indicates how recent it is that women are finding their intimate experiences of sex, love, marriage, childbirth, and divorce credibly captured in fiction.

Beginning with Alix Kates Shulman's *Memoirs of an Ex-Prom Queen* (1972), a popular novel growing out of the new feminist consciousness, women readers have been relishing books that invite them into the world of the feminine as they know it to be. *The Women's Room* (1977) by Marilyn French became a metaphor for an entire generation seeking to identify the feminine as profoundly separate from masculine experience. But breathing the freer air of 1983, the olympian Ruth revolts with demonic humor against the "Litany of the Good Wife" in Fay Weldon's *The Life and Loves of a She-Devil*.

A forty-six-year-old woman, married for twenty-five years, carried a book into her first meeting with an attorney to discuss divorce. After the interview, when he asked pleasantly about her reading, she answered: "It's Margaret Drabble's new novel, *The Radiant Way*. A friend recommended that I read it to see what happens to a woman when her husband wants a divorce after twenty-five years of marriage."

To see their lives revealed in print is still a fresh new joy for women. When poet Muriel Rukeyser asked in 1973, "What would happen if one woman told the truth about her life?" she answered, "The world would split open."

For *Divorced Women, New Lives*, forty-five real women, not literary characters, tell the truth about their marriages from wedding day to beyond divorce. They speak openly about marital conflict, the pain of divorce,

9

the struggle of gaining personal and social identity, and their pride in new achievements. These women have survived deep hurt and a range of obstacles. Yet they have moved beyond depression and anger to achieve personal peace and fulfillment in their work. Their accounts are detailed so that women experiencing divorce will have another way, outside of reading novels and diaries, to identify with women, like themselves, who have succeeded. Within our own lifetime, women have trusted such personal stories only to their journals.

Listening to the tapes of these interviews, one hears, for example, the voices of women exposing feelings similar to those that Sophie Tolstoy, in 1887, confided to her diary: "I am so used to living not my own life, but the life of Lyova and the children, that I feel I have wasted my day if I haven't done something for them. . . . It is sad that my emotional dependence on the man I love should have killed so much of my energy and ability; there was certainly once a great deal of energy in me. . . ."

Hidden in a journal, the words of Sophie Tolstoy were of no benefit to her contemporaries. Yet a century later, Tolstoy's same tensions are echoed in the voice of Jessica Schumann, who speaks openly about her divorce: "My ex-husband is a physicist who never saw my talent as a writer as being equal to his. I wrote in the kitchen so that I would always be available to him and the children. I made my writing secondary to everything else. But Theodore thought it was all right for me to write because my success was a reflection of him, as long as it didn't interfere with my cleaning the bathroom."

Jessica Schumann also keeps a journal but does not depend upon it as an emotional outlet as women once did. A century after Sophie Tolstoy, women are freer about expressing what they have done and who they really are. Nonetheless they feel isolated, lonely, and confused during the crisis of divorce and seek identification with ex-wives who have weathered its turmoil. For this reason, divorced women who have built independent lives tell their stories for this book so that other women will find hope in them and develop the determination to forge their own new paths. They want women in similar situations to benefit from their hard-won advice.

Each of the women interviewed, for example, values the role of mentor, either because she treasures a strong feminine guide in her own life or because she regrets never having had one. From experience, she knows that a mentor need not be on the scene to be a positive influence. One woman claims, "Germaine Greer changed my life with *The Female Eunuch*. Reading that book assured me that I wasn't crazy for thinking the way I did. For the first time, I didn't try to squelch the inner voice prodding me that I shouldn't be satisfied with the way my life was." But in a different way, another woman continues the legacy of a trusting mentor who offered her the most basic security: "I will always remember that kind woman who gave me money when I had left my husband and started a new job. She never expected to have it returned. Since then, I have tried in whatever way I can to support women who need help."

In whatever way they can, all the women interviewed for *Divorced Women, New Lives* want to help women through the process of divorce and then onward to leading creative, productive lives. To do so, they responded in an extended conversation to a series of questions that had not been given to them in advance of our meetings. The questions followed the chronology of the woman's life, beginning somewhere before her wedding day:

"What did you do before you were married?"

"How did you value that work?"

"Did you work after you married?"

"If not, how did you feel about giving it up?"

"Will you describe the circumstances of your marriage?"

"Did you make a conscious decision to marry your husband?"

"What did your parents think about the match?"

"Will you describe your wedding day?"

"What was life like with your husband?"

"Did you share the same interests and values?"

"When did conflicts arise?"

"Did you want to save the marriage?"

"What did you do to save the marriage?"

"Did you have professional counseling?"

"Were you in therapy?"

"What was the lowest point in the marriage?"

"How soon after that were you divorced?"

"What did you give up by no longer being Mrs.____?"

"What were your personal risks?"

"What were your gains?"

"When you decided to divorce, were you clear about your next step?"

"At that time, how did you feel about your future?"

"What was your self-worth?"

"What were your goals?"

"Will you describe your emotional state through the process of divorce?"

"Whom did you depend upon for emotional support?"

"How did you draw strength on a day-to-day basis?"

"What was your process of renewal?"

"How important was the financial settlement to your fulfilling your goals?"

"Did you fulfill your goals?"

"How do you describe yourself today?"

"Knowing what you now know, would you do anything different about your life?"

"At the lowest point of your marriage, did you ever think you would get where you are now?"

"What is your present relationship with your husband?"

"Were you influenced by the women's movement?"

"Would you remarry?"

"What are you most proud of about yourself?"

"What is your advice to other women who are struggling with divorce?"

Listing these questions conveys the impression of a stilted, linear interview, whereas following circuitous paths, the women responded candidly, sometimes tearfully, with detailed stories and often bemused reflections. Recalling personal incidents from the past, they often paused to share fresh insights about either themselves, their husbands, or divorce in general. They are warm and witty women, mostly unknown to each other but united by a shared adversity and a commitment to helping other women not merely to survive divorce, but to triumph over its devastating effects. They want to tell what they were aching to ask women in the same situation who had gone before them. Remembering their own feelings of isolation, they want women in the process of divorce to gain confidence from these personal accounts so that the world of fiction and published diaries is not their only means of emotional identification and self-discovery.

Readers looking for easy answers will not find them here, however. "Divorce is a drastic measure," each woman says in her own vocabulary. "It is not for the faint of heart." It is not the intention of this book, nor of the women interviewed, to advocate divorce. Many of them endured terrible marriages for decades of their lives before making that decision. For the woman who is committed to her marriage, breaking free from the words of her wedding vows is a scarring experience. But when the marriage ultimately diminishes her personal integrity and the only alternative is to witness her psychological and emotional destruction, she takes the "drastic measure." Although divorce was their last alternative, these women want others to know that it is possible to find peace and fulfillment after it occurs.

Also included in this book are insights garnered from private interviews with attorneys, psychologists, financial consultants, and credit executives who were willing to offer practical advice to divorced women based on their professional experience. But the main purpose of *Divorced Women, New Lives* is to offer readers a direct expression of the lives of divorced women without interruption for polemics, statistics, politics, or academic studies. The research is the interviews themselves, as divorced women are the best articulators of what divorced women think, feel, and suffer. Themes, insights, and conclusions that emerge result from patterns suggested by the interviews. A substantial body of literature exists on divorce and its legal, economic, and social effects on women and children. What is lacking is a book where ordinary women speak from the heart so that others who are leveled by divorce will find the courage to shape their own futures. The purpose here is to connect women with each other through the ancient practice of personal narrative.

A woman who has resumed an interrupted college education after her divorce studies in a library carrel close to the holdings on women. "When I am tired of studying, I rifle the shelves trying to find success stories about women. I know and believe the evidence that shows where culture and society have gone wrong with women. And certainly I don't want to read any more about the mistakes I have made. I know what they are, and they are behind me. I simply want to know about women like myself who go on to lead successful lives." *Divorced Women, New Lives* is intended to satisfy that need.

Although this book focuses on the problems of

women and divorce, it is not my intention to convey an antimale attitude. Most of the women interviewed, in fact, would agree to marry the right man; some are now very happy in second marriages. But when a husband and wife divorce, each has a perspective that makes the other vulnerable. A similar project could be undertaken to interview divorced men in order to uncover the similarities of their experiences and to see if they are different from the hardships that women face.

Finally, I did not choose to interview women who have made their divorce their *raison d'être*. Reminiscent of Miss Havisham in Dickens's *Great Expectations*, who sat for years in her decaying wedding gown, they too memorialize the precise second of their betrayal. How are some women, even in oppressive circumstances, able to define their lives after divorce when others remain immobilized by anger, almost proud that they lack inner freedom? The answer seems to lie in a woman's willingness to undertake self-examination, review her upbringing, question social conditioning, define her strengths, exorcise personal demons, and accept responsibility for making choices. For example, the Havisham model of righteousness requires a woman to be unflinching in her conviction that she was wronged, refusing ever to question how she also contributed to the failure of her expectations. Women with this mindset doom themselves to a crippling fate because they live to blame others for the condition they are in. They remain passive victims, refusing to grow from their suffering.

In an essay entitled "Self-Respect," Joan Didion

writes: "To be driven back upon oneself is an uneasy affair at best . . . [but] . . . it seems to me now the one condition necessary to the beginnings of real self-respect. . . . However long we postpone it, we eventually lie down alone in that notoriously uncomfortable bed, the one we make ourselves. Whether or not we sleep in it depends, of course, on whether or not we respect ourselves."

Applying Didion's terms to the situation of divorced women reveals that those who become independent have had the courage to fall back upon themselves to discover, without self-deception, who they really are. To do this requires a "habit of mind that can never be faked but can be developed, trained, coaxed forth." Such introspection promises pain, but from it a divorced woman will learn not to base her self-worth on satisfying the expectations of others. She no longer pays the price of losing self-respect by accommodating herself to what others think, absorbing their judgment of what she should want and how she should act. Consequently, she assumes responsibility for her future by making her own deliberate choices, aware that risk is always an inherent factor. Not lingering with dreams of her wedding gown, she dares to cut new patterns. Sara Teasdale's "Advice to a Girl" can never be learned too late: "No one worth possessing can be quite possessed."

Women who find fulfillment after divorce also have faith in life, whatever its problems. Shortly after having separated from her husband, one woman recalls a Saturday morning when she was happy to send off her children to ice-skating lessons because she was almost too sad to get through the day. Crying in bed, she suddenly remembered that the next day was Easter, and she had not yet arranged the children's baskets. She immediately dressed and left for a candy store. Giving in to her sadness was not worth sacrificing the joy of watching her children find their baskets on Sunday morning. This attitude is typical of women who know, on one hand, that divorce requires a mourning time, but who will not allow grief and anger to stop their celebration of life's fleeting pleasures.

On the day she moved out of their house while her husband was lecturing in Tokyo, Jessica Schumann watched her furniture and paintings being carried from rooms where they had been at home for twenty years. One of the moving crew, noticing her sudden wave of tears, asked if he could be of help. Learning that she was leaving her husband, he rescued her with the miracle of a cliché: "Ah, hell. Life is too short to be unhappy."

"Damn right," she answered. And went on packing.

CHAPTER 2

Wedding Marches

My career was the central focus of everything I did.
Now, my life centers around my husband.
Grace Kelly
Look
February 5, 1957

A woman who succeeds in building an independent life and achieving peace of mind after divorce was like any other bride. She married for reasons of the heart or pocketbook; to solve the problems of pregnancy, silence the nagging of anxious parents, or satisfy her romantic destiny as wife and mother. On her wedding day, she was committed to making her marriage work, not simply to trying it out. She was not a maverick who bargained at the altar: "If this marriage isn't successful, then I'll start college, go to law school, open a business, write, paint, become a corporate executive, a magazine editor, a pricey real estate developer, a financial analyst; I'll run for office, finish a doctorate, or concentrate on advancing my own career."

To name such goals is not easy for divorced women. They struggle through difficult journeys in order to chart new courses for their lives. With hindsight, they tell the stories of these journeys better than anyone else, beginning with the wedding, not necessarily acknowledged as the first mistake.

Some divorced women recognize that their idea of marriage was basically incompatible with seeking personal fulfillment outside of the roles of wife and mother. A character in Edith Wharton's 1922 novel, *The Age of Innocence*, identifies this tradition by describing a young bride whose "only use of the liberty she supposed herself to possess would be to lay it on the altar of her wifely devotion." But brides of later decades were just as programmed to be self-effacing. During the fifties and early sixties, when men and women agreed that wives should be passive partners in marriage, the unapproachable Grace Kelly exquisitely disguised the reality of women's inferior status.

Jessica Schumann, forty-nine, who now earns her living as a writer of poetry and fiction, left behind any urge to create for herself when she married Theodore. She recalls sublimating her awareness of the double message of the Grace Kelly image when her father twenty-two years ago cleared his throat and said, "Princess, you've been dating that fellow for three years now. Don't you think I should ask his intentions?" Jessica thought she was freely choosing Theodore to be her husband but now realizes that when her father said that it was time for her to marry, she simply agreed.

Eyes brimming with tears, Rose Lewis also recalls that her dream to be in the theater went unfulfilled because it was a "woman's duty to marry." After graduating from college in 1948, she spent two years studying acting in Manhattan. "Dad always said, 'Am I going to have an old maid on my hands?' I felt it was a sin not to be married at twenty-one. Even after I was engaged, I considered breaking it. I never thought to continue my acting career because it simply would not have looked right for my husband. My marriage lasted thirty-five years, but I still don't know why I ever married him."

Rose describes her marriage as unraveling like a "dime novel" when she learned about Leonard's affair. "But I'm happy now. I'm no longer a square. I can manage money and make decisions about my life. Dad and Leonard always had implied that I was a sweet girl, 'but really there's not much there.'"

The success that is rewarding to divorced women does not always include career advancement, public recognition, or financial achievement. For some, like Rose Lewis, to gain confidence and autonomy are miracles enough. For others, the challenge is to discover and develop untapped talents so that they can confidently define and pursue their own new horizons.

Parental pressure on daughters to marry, such as that experienced by Jessica Schumann and Rose Lewis, can be especially threatening if it is combined with the subtle persuasion of religious values. Shielded and succored by home and church, Bridget Downey, for example, was eagerly obedient to serve at the "altar of her wifely devotion."

Now a college sophomore at age forty-seven with four teenagers, Bridget accepted Patrick's proposal on their third date. "It was a marriage made in heaven," Bridget muses ironically, "because we were introduced by Patrick's brother, a priest. The sun rose and set on Father Ignatius, and so I thought his brother would have to be as wonderful." For an added bonus, Patrick, a stockbroker in his late twenties, showed promise of buying Bridget the china and crystal that she had grown accustomed to at home.

Even though she had worked in her family's business by managing money and employees, Bridget thought she needed to have a husband to take care of her. Introspectively she comments: "I had a great deal of responsibility in the business and even opened and managed a branch store in a new shopping mall, but I thought of myself as being very ordinary. I was twenty-one; it was 1962. Patrick would be an excellent provider, and my parents approved."

Bridget knows that she ignored early signals, even before their wedding, of Patrick's bisexuality because "nice girls did not think or talk about things like that." At her Catholic all-girls' high school, Bridget had been a member of the "Fighting Sixty-ninth," a national movement enlisting young women to promise that they would not sin against the sixth and ninth commandments. Bridget was relieved during their engagement that Patrick's sexual demands were "always respectful." But after their marriage, she lived in misery as Patrick entertained lovers in their home. Bridget also endured his physical abuse because she never thought she could make it on her own to support four children, one of them with Down's syndrome and another with severe learning disabilities.

Bridget's final humiliation occurred when she was forced to find protection in a shelter for physically abused women while Patrick enjoyed a split-level with his lover. Only then did she finally emancipate herself and her children from this debilitating marriage and acknowledge her self-worth by setting her sights on earning a bachelor's degree. As the result of a project for an anthropology class, she has established a self-help group for wives of bisexuals and plans to pursue graduate studies in public policy.

Bridget's passivity is not unusual, although her example is extreme. Women have long believed that a ring and a blessing will make a perfect marriage. In order to live the American dream as a fulfilled wife, mother, and homemaker, women will admit to having denied serious reservations about their future husbands. And a woman's insecurities about achieving her own career goals and economic independence are not necessarily alleviated by her level of education.

A graduate of a prep school and a women's liberal arts college, Isabel Howell, forty-three, an artist and owner of a small gallery before her marriage, dated her husband for two years and knew his womanizing well. Still, she married John, naively confident that he could be reformed. "I was fascinated because John knew wines, read widely, conversed well, and had lived in Europe for a number of years. Besides that, he was on his way up in banking. I thought he could take care of me better than anyone I had ever dated. I was twenty-eight, and thirty loomed ahead as terrible as fifty! I felt pressure from everybody."

From the early days of her marriage, Isabel spent creative energy trying to sculpt herself into the perfect Galatea, smoothing out her flaws in an effort to keep John focused only on her. She also saw a psychiatrist twice a week in order to withstand John's constant criticism. She confides, "We had decent sex before marriage, but not after. It was a classic case of separating the wife and the whore." But since divorcing three years ago, Isabel has regained her psychic health, and her once dormant art career is flourishing. Her paintings sell for six thousand dollars and have been exhibited in East Coast galleries.

Isabel's claim of feeling pressure from everybody to marry is repeated by other women who gain self-knowledge and leave stifling marriages. Wanting the approval of parents and friends, they marry what fashion dictates as their perfect match. Consequently the couple lives in an unreal world: having married her "dream man," the wife accommodates her husband's fantasy by playing the part she must in order to gain his approval. Early in marriage women may have fleeting insights into the cycle of such counterfeit behavior, but years may pass before they have the confidence to halt the charade. Isabel Howell knew after six months that she had married a fantasy but did not break free for twelve more years.

Doris Minton, fifty, now vice-president of finances for a small New England university, had the same recognition even before the wedding invitations were printed, yet she stayed with her husband for twenty-two years before seriously pursuing her own academic career. Similar to Isabel, she married her ideal: a seminary student with a quick mind and wit, a young man worthy of her own intelligence. Arguments flourished between the glib bride and bridegroom as wedding plans escalated. Aware of tension, Doris's mother inquired, "You're still getting married, aren't you?" With hindsight, Doris knows her answer reflected the truth: "Oh, yes, Mother. You have already ordered the invitations." Rationalizing that all young couples experienced anxiety before their wedding, and not wanting to cause her parents distress, Doris remained stubborn that the ceremony would indeed take place.

Doris was married only a year when, standing pregnant against the kitchen sink, she wondered how she could continue to live with a man whom she judged to be self-righteous and insensitive, while the rest of the world saw him as a decent, high-minded ministerial student. Doris explains, "I decided that there must be something wrong with me because you just didn't divorce young men who were going to be ministers." And so she resolved to be the absolutely perfect, traditional wife. Although she had her academic career on hold until Andy was ordained and then finished his doctorate, Doris did not feel thwarted by this decision. Her priority was to correct her behavior by overlooking Andy's surliness so that she could be true to her marriage vows and establish a happy family life. "I realized that I had made a terrible choice," Doris admits, "but I could not see myself making a commitment and backing out of it."

For twenty-two years Doris stayed determined to

save her marriage, but even with children, few days were really happy. Most of the time she felt like a "trapped animal," especially toward the end when Andy lost all self-respect and spent a sabbatical sitting in his underwear, drunk, in the living room. When they finally separated, Doris finished a long postponed doctorate and began a successful academic career at age forty-three. She is most proud of the fact that she has four splendid children. But if Doris had the opportunity to replay her life, she would call the printer and cancel the wedding invitations.

It may be hard to differentiate between the ordinary trepidation a woman experiences before a wedding and the anxiety she has when she is truly afraid of the marriage. But the deep fears of Stephanie Vogel were not ambiguous. A college senior in 1965, Stephanie prayed at the altar, "God forgive me. I'm entering into this marriage with reservations, but I'm too scared not to do it." Stephanie was in love—"if we can accept Freud's definition that to be in love is a temporary form of insanity"—with Larry, an engineering student. She was pregnant but would not consider an abortion. Moreover, she had reneged on a decision to accept a place in a home for single mothers willing to give up their infants for adoption. Stephanie asked God's forgiveness because of her firm moral conviction that she needed to know more about herself before committing to marriage.

For twenty years Stephanie and Larry lived in tension, trying to understand each other's needs. Stephanie was popular in their small town, north of Boston, as a free-lance writer who championed environmental causes, but she never pursued a definite professional career because Larry did not support her success. When Stephanie was honored for her efforts on behalf of conservation at a dinner recognizing the town's movers and shakers, a toothache prevented Larry from attending. Stephanie tried for a few more years to adapt her behavior to Larry's comfort zone. But after watching the slow death of a very good friend, both decided that life was too precious to continue living in unresolved conflict. Stephanie finished graduate school and then filed for divorce. Now she is a psychologist with a growing private practice. She looks forward to writing a book and marrying again.

Stephanie had always been counseled by her working-class mother not to marry too young because "good girls don't settle on one guy." But Lorraine Lucas, who also loved her large, extended working-class family, was cheered on by them not to finish college and "to settle down." After only one semester at state college, she married a senior whom "I figured I had a lifetime to learn to love." Their raucous wedding reception was so much fun that Lorraine didn't want to leave, but besides that, "Ted was drunk as a skunk." For six months Lorraine worked as a file clerk before becoming pregnant: "I wanted desperately to be a mother. That was my only career. Now I would have different options about choosing to be a single parent, and I don't think I would hesitate about not being married."

By age thirty Lorraine felt starved for a larger world and began taking college courses, a need Ted failed to understand. She had only one class a semester, but Ted could not tolerate anything about her student life. When she was typing a final paper, he raged, "I would like to keep you locked up in a closet until I want you, and then put you back. If I had known you were going to be like this, I never would have married you."

The next time Lorraine sat at her desk, Ted strode from the bedroom in his Jockey briefs, ripped the paper from the typewriter, and raped her. Ted regarded Lorraine so much as his possession that this scene occurred a few more times. When Lorraine separated from Ted, she also had to endure the barbs of her unsupporting family. But now she laughs when recalling her grandmother tearing at her own clothes and shouting, "How can you leave him, Lorraine, when you have such beautiful china?"

Lorraine's luck changed when she was able to retain a lawyer after winning one thousand dollars in a church raffle. She kept creditors at bay, enrolled full-time in a local college, and finished her bachelor's degree as the divorced mother of four young sons. She paid her tuition by cleaning houses and fed her boys with the help of food stamps. For a time, she lived on welfare. At age thirty-seven Lorraine teaches at a community college while writing a doctoral dissertation in psychology and looking for a permanent position on a university faculty. She also is available for patients as a counselor in a gynecologist's office.

Married in 1969, Lorraine is chagrined that she was not aware of Betty Friedan's *The Feminine Mystique* (1963), which anticipated and defined her problems.

But other women who married at that time also admit to having had negative or selective responses to the women's movement. The romantic counterrevolutionary image of Grace Kelly surrendering to her prince dominated their consciousness rather than the revolutionary reality of women questioning their preordained roles. When planning marriage in the sixties, the rare woman truly heard the rising voices of feminism. But when deciding to divorce, the same women who had given no heed to feminist writing then depended upon it for clarification and support. Nancy Stewart is one of them.

Now the manager of her own insurance company, clearing an annual profit of $125,000 for herself, Nancy remembers her wedding as the fulfillment of a dream. "My mother was hysterical because I was twenty-one and unmarried, a nursery school teacher living by myself in Washington, D.C." When Nancy met Bill Stewart in 1964, she knew he was the answer to her mother's urgent prayers: a graduate of an Ivy League law school and a prestigious eastern college. Nancy admits that she pursued Bill, "absolutely willed him," even while recognizing his drinking problems and attending Al-Anon meetings without his knowledge. The night they returned from their wedding trip, Nancy knew her marriage was hopeless, but she blamed only herself for the glaring problems. Having landed her prince, an unhappy ending, she reasoned, could be only her mistake.

Even after divorcing Bill, Nancy still assumed blame for the breakup because, ostensibly, Bill was everything that her Brahman mother had wanted for her. By choosing not to be Mrs. Stewart, Nancy felt she was giving up "everything I had believed in as being wonderful." With studied seriousness, she sighs and adds, "But I survived my stupidity."

Nancy received only fifty dollars a week from Bill, who enjoyed golf, a Brooks Brothers wardrobe, and expensive Scotch. But she managed to keep the facade of their marriage so perfect that she had no excuse to leave him that would be acceptable to her stern New England parents. Even Bill's alcoholism and physical abuse of her would be construed by them as her fault. Nancy remembers cowering behind the furnace one night, worrying about the children in bed, waiting until dawn for his violence to expend itself.

Nancy returned to her family the day she discovered Bill was intimate with another woman, the only breach of promise she knew her father would recognize. Immediately he insisted that she get a job in a local dress shop. "I thought that was tough medicine at the time," Nancy says, wincing, "but it was probably the best thing for me to do. I had been so used to camouflaging my personal problems that it was a relief to be able to talk to people and be myself." The job also built Nancy's confidence and allowed her a financial cushion to prepare for a real estate license. Hired by a real estate office that also sold insurance, Nancy found she liked insurance better and did well at selling. Within a few years she had established enough credit to borrow money to open her own insurance agency. Now remarried to a successful physician, Nancy chooses to maintain expenses for herself and three children, all college students: "I never want to ask a man for money again. I pay absolutely everything for myself and kids, prep school and college tuitions included."

Wedding story after wedding story, regardless of the bride's socioeconomic status or level of education, reveals a woman who awakens from cramped quarters to recognize the emotional damage that is caused by surrendering to a husband's dream of what she should be. Furthermore, she has permitted his dream of her to exist because he represents, for whatever reason, all that promises to make her whole and complete. To live as a captured princess is to exist as the object of someone else's imagination. Brides who awaken to this reality free themselves to become creators.

One of these creators is Harriet Loeb, now in her third term as an elected representative to the Albany legislature from upstate New York. But Harriet admits that previous to her political career, her knowledge of her city was limited to the merchandise carried by the major department stores and exclusive shops. And she could not even find her own way among them, as she was chauffeured daily by the same taxi driver. Harriet had ten expired learner's permits because she was terrified to drive. Candidly, she describes herself as "the epitome of the Jewish American princess. My conversation and life rotated around what the housekeeper did and did not do. From the standpoint of many, I led a privileged life, but money and things are not enough."

At age thirty Harriet married a resident in neurosurgery at a New York City hospital. Born in northern

Michigan, the daughter of divorced parents, Harriet had a strict upbringing as an orthodox Jew in a foster home and had attended parochial schools. By the time she was ten, Harriet had read *Madame Bovary*, for the library was her refuge from a lonely childhood. "I jogged before anyone knew what to call it because the library was three miles away, and I was always back and forth." But despite her obvious intelligence, Harriet's father would not hear of her going to college; instead she attended business school for a year before working as a dance instructor for one of a national chain of studios in Detroit, where soon she was writing sales packages that caught the eye of the corporate president. She was promoted to sales for a Park Avenue studio and then transferred to Boston, "where I introduced the authentic cha-cha and mambo to Back Bay. Boston women never had to worry that I would poach their husbands or boyfriends. I was safe because I never dated non-Jews."

But at age twenty-seven in 1956, Harriet was unmarried and knew that "a nice Jewish boy didn't want to take someone who was in the dance business home to meet Mother." So she changed jobs and worked in the accounts department of one of New York City's largest discount houses, where she completely changed their credit system. When the boss offered her a magnanimous five-dollar bonus at Christmas, she was insulted and quit. Harriet was successful in similar positions until meeting Stanley Loeb, whom she describes as being "bright, articulate, and like a rock; besides that he was older than I, and I needed a father." When his residency was completed, they married and moved to Syracuse where Stanley would practice.

During their marriage, Harriet never thought to work, even though she's a "Leo and can do anything." She refers to herself as having been *"Frau Doktor* because doctor's wives could only be social workers or schoolteachers. If they worked at anything else, it would look as if their husbands weren't successful."

Ironically, Harriet was "reborn at forty" because her childhood days in northern Michigan had instilled in her a love of nature and the land. Consequently she was drawn to attend a series of university-sponsored lectures in the Mohawk region given by prominent researchers on the threat of waste disposal. Appalled by what she heard, she invited to her home friends who were also sensitive to environmental issues and formed a coalition that became vocal in the community on the dangers of pollutants. Soon Harriet was writing hundreds of reports, testifying in Washington, speaking in neighborhood seminars and for courses at local colleges and high schools on issues of the environment. Harriet's name became a local household word. She also got her driver's license. As her star rose in the community, Harriet admitted the emptiness that she felt with her marriage. "Stanley always said my life would change once I learned to drive." Then she adds with a twinkle, "But he didn't know how dramatically."

Brides of the fifties and sixties, like Harriet Loeb and Nancy Stewart, more often than not measured their self-worth by the promise of the young men whom they captured, rather than by their own intelligence. In prefeminist days, few young women knew what they wanted for themselves or even thought to probe the question, "Who am I?"

Nina Hibbert, fifty, now a psychiatric social worker in a large urban hospital, acknowledges that she lived "in a fantasy world for most of my college life. I came from an academic family, so when I started college I had in mind marrying a lawyer, teacher, or clergyman. On the very first day of classes, I met another freshman who said he wanted to be a college professor. To understand why I thought our relationship was made in heaven, you have to know that the day before I left for school I had attended a family wedding. One of my relatives, who is happily married, said to me, 'Look out for whom you meet. Look at us, we dated from our freshman year!' And I thought, That's the kind of life I'd like to have. But I answered, 'Oh, no, I'm not going to college to meet somebody. I'm going to study.' Yet in the registration line the next day when I met this attractive young man who wanted to be a professor, I thought our relationship had been preordained, really a blessing. For the next four years, I dated no one else."

After Will Hibbert earned his doctorate, he moved from campus to campus, always as an assistant professor, because he alienated faculty and students with his pugnacious, aggressive manner. Nina reflects that she chose "to marry Will because of the role he would assume, not because of his personal values or our deep compatibility. Will had hang-ups that kept him from succeeding. His contracts were never renewed because he had a need to be at odds with people. He had been an abused child. After years in the psychiatric field, I know that some can recover and others can't. Even as a college student he was constantly at war with authority, but I guess I chose to overlook that fact. As a young faculty family, we had the life-style and status that I had always wanted, but Will was a consistent public embarrassment because he would take on authority figures on campus and in town."

Besides his need to be aggressive, Will had a penchant for spending the couple's hard-earned money. Nina continues to analyze, "He had an enormous desire to own things, but if I tried to persuade him against spending money, he perceived me as the bad mother who wouldn't give to him. We both earned. He spent, and I was supposed to make ends meet." Rather than serve a series of part-time jobs, Nina decided to finish a master's degree in social work before filing for divorce. "For years, we tried to work out our problems in family therapy. It was so hard for me because I would see people progress in therapy, but not in my own family. But some abused children are just so scarred that they can't recover. Only when I worked professionally in the field myself was I able to piece together my husband's case. But more accurately, I actually blinded myself to his problems because I wasn't financially prepared to leave him and support the children. I wanted to save our marriage because I was panicked about being by myself, even though I was more competent than he. I could tolerate his leaving, but not my own. Even at the end, he was the bad guy and left. Only after psychoanalysis did I see my own participation in all of this."

But when they had met as college freshmen eighteen years earlier, Nina was primarily concerned with "marrying a kind of life-style, and Will Hibbert's desire to be a professor appealed to me. I never thought about the larger questions. I never thought about who I really was or, for that matter, who he really was."

While this thinking prevailed among young women during the fifties and early sixties, it is not yet obsolete. Very perplexing are the yuppie brides of the seventies willing to step back and hold the ladder that they once had a foot on. Different from young women of the eighties, they do remember when career opportunities for women were circumscribed. Yet they will completely abdicate their own career development to pursue traditional female goals.

In 1976 Margaret Peterson graduated cum laude as an English major from a metropolitan university. But after three hard years employed as a copy writer in an advertising firm, she reveals, "I simply wanted to marry. I had a great future, but I wanted only a ring, a house, and a baby. Scott kept telling me what a brilliant policy analyst he was, and he came along at the right time. I sublimated all the signals in our relationship that indicated our basic incompatibility. I pretended it didn't matter when he took me to a pawnshop to buy my engagement ring. It was a real Woody Allen vignette. The pawnbroker put a ring on each one of his hairy fingers and said, 'Which one takes your fancy?'"

Exchanging wedding vows, Scott said, "I, Margaret, take you, Scott—" The minister interrupted to center him: "You're Scott; this is Margaret." But Scott could never recall the telling incident. Romance did not exist in Margaret and Scott's marriage, just hard-nosed practicality. They invested every cent of their money into renovating an old farmhouse an hour's drive from the city. "We thought it would be fun to redo," admits Margaret, "but it was absolute hell. We were ill-equipped financially, physically, and emotionally." In fact, Margaret claims the house was a metaphor for her marriage: "For months we lived with a giant hole in the wall; it helped us not to focus on each other. We were building a house, not a home."

Scott invested extra money into buying heavy tools and equipment that Margaret claims he didn't even know how to use. "We never took a trip; we sacrificed everything for the house. We pretended to be so close, but the only things we shared were blisters and cuts."

Then the house needed to have a child, but pregnancy was elusive for Margaret. For seven years she went through fertility studies, therapy, and surgery without success: "I was devastated that my body would not work, but we always knew that adoption was an option." Christmas week, when the child they were to adopt was to be born, Margaret confronted Scott with evidence that he was having an affair with a co-worker and that he was also the father of her two-month-old son. "Even then, Scott didn't understand why I couldn't be practical and tolerate this situation, so that in a few days I would also have a baby."

After their separation, Margaret lacked self-confidence and the power of concentration to resume a professional career. Her first job was to keep the dressing rooms tidy in a discount dress store: "But I was happy to pick up pins from the floors because I could see what I was accomplishing." Then for six months she worked as a cocktail waitress in order to pay for therapy: "I knew I had to understand why I married a man who expected me to be so accommodating. After a year of therapy, I began to think about taking some risks and enrolled in an eight-week program to be certified as a paralegal. I was so focused on achieving my goal that I suddenly realized it was the first time I hadn't thought about being rescued by another man. I had some sense of rescuing myself." After working for one year as a paralegal in a large law firm, Margaret developed enough confidence to apply for law school. Now a senior, Margaret is determined never again to stifle her own development in order to be the ultimate helpmate.

Margaret's recovery from the trauma of divorce was compounded by the fact that she and Scott were unable to have children. "There are certain aspects of divorce," she contends, "that you can conquer by putting yourself in a better economic position. But I can be on top of the world and still feel the tap on the shoulder, the reminder of what I don't have, a child. When I was first divorced, people would say, 'Well, thank God you don't have any children.' And I would feel very hurt by that remark. People in general are just not sensitive about infertility." Margaret describes another tap on the shoulder: "The first time I played Scruples with friends, I picked the card that says something like 'If you discovered that your partner was infertile, would you leave him or her?' Conventional wisdom says you're lucky not to have children if you have been divorced, but when the biological clock is ticking, and you've been through seven years of fertility therapy and three years of adoption procedures, it complicates your feelings after divorce. Not too many people are sensitive to this issue, and I keep bumping into it. Divorce is one thing; infertility is another. Combined, they are powerful personal issues to sort out."

Women like Margaret Peterson begin to sort out their divorces and create new lives because they are willing to ask themselves why they married the men that they did. In facing the original terms of their marriage, they free themselves from self-deception by acknowledging that they did make a choice. They try to get a sharpened focus on the wedding in order to understand their complicity, however unintentional, in the breakdown of the marital relationship. Although details vary, these women expose their emotional dependency, fear of loneliness or social disapproval, or romantic assumption that a ceremony would exempt them from experiencing the ordinary problems of life. Whether they are helped by therapy or are their own guides, divorced women who eventually bring purpose and meaning to their lives rescue themselves by self-confrontation. They name their needs and accept themselves as fallible human beings. For them, divorce is not simply a trauma to pass through on the way to another marriage, but a terrible experience that must be understood if they are to avoid further personal devastation.

Maria Graham, divorced for five years, squarely admits that it takes two to make a bad marriage. The only daughter in a household of six children, her mother and her father, a machinist, worried constantly about money. Yet her parents would not permit her to work at any job until after high school graduation. Maria's mother, a compulsive overeater, was the daughter of a violent alcoholic father and the wife of a quiet alcoholic as well. Maria's mother lived with fear and restrained her daughter from exploring too much of life.

But at age twenty Maria was a chemistry technician in a private lab used by sixteen pathologists who respected her ability. After mastering the details of the job, she also attended modeling school and was soon hired as a part-time teacher to supplement her salary in the lab. For her age in 1964 Maria was a financial success, earning more than twenty thousand dollars a year. She bought a secondhand Cadillac convertible and was in no hurry to marry. She identified her family's poverty with her father's "ineffectuality" and therefore decided to marry only a "strong-willed" man, "words," says Maria, "that I have gained only in retrospect."

Therefore, she was immediately attracted to flamboyant Sebastian Graham, a construction engineer whose boats, cars, and monogrammed shirts proved he was beyond poverty. Prior to their marriage, Sebastian had attended meetings of Alcoholics Anonymous but defined his own drinking in a way that released him of any obligation to continue with the program. Sebastian and Maria drank hard together: "For seven years we had an emotionally sick marriage." Maria remembers "all-night battles that emptied me of all emotion. Our lives became more and more shabby."

Maria joined AA and was willing to make an inventory of her resentments. It was a while before she could forgive her parents, particularly her mother, for fostering fears in her that bred emotional dependency and caused her to dismiss qualities of gentleness in a man. But she also grew in compassion for her mother, who had often witnessed brutal fights between her own parents, causing her to project inarticulate fears onto her daughter. But Maria, at least, now names her own demons and deals with pain in positive and not self-destructive ways. For example, she resurrected the gutsy young woman who managed a medical laboratory.

After her separation, Maria could not afford to enroll in courses relevant to building self-esteem or discovering new careers. Earning money with small catering jobs and by tending bar in a neighborhood restaurant, she took to heart advice offered by an executive woman whom she heard on a television talk show. "It was a slow afternoon, so right there at the bar I made a list of everything I had ever accomplished from the time I was ten years old. I applied the same process that I had learned in AA about understanding my emotional needs to uncovering my skills." The list endorsed Maria's strength in property management, for she and Sebastian had dabbled in real estate before losing their money to alcohol.

Determined not to work in real estate, Maria surveyed her environment and approached a nearby state university to see if a need existed there for a property manager. The personnel office was convinced that she fit the requirements to be the manager of a campus guest house and faculty club, a position that had not yet been advertised.

Maria earns an annual salary of thirty-five thousand dollars and supervises a staff of twenty-four. Her confidence keeps blossoming as her responsibilities grow: "As I take more risks, I discover abilities I didn't know I had, and my fear evaporates." Maria respects herself too much to become enmeshed in another debilitating relationship. But until she was willing to chart and forgive the forces that shaped her own needs, Maria admits that she would never have been able to take the helm of her life into her own hands.

Divorced women are able to assume responsibility for their own lives when they risk the vulnerability to ask themselves why they married the men that they did. They free themselves to act independently when they understand that their reasons for choosing their husbands can often be better understood in the light of their own needs and conditioning. Such insight brings self-confidence rather than the uncertainty that results when a woman has not examined her previous ways of responding and falls into a pattern of either repeated or passive behavior.

When divorced women speak about their weddings, they attempt to explain their reasons for marrying the men they did. But without resisting introspection, some simply do say, "We were in love." Pensively, Naomi Davis remarks, "We were college sweethearts. Even now, I'm not sure I would do things differently. At that point, it was all just right." As a romantic young bride, Naomi always thought she could count on her husband to be interested in her accomplishments. Never would she have predicted that twenty years later he would detain himself at the office to miss the opening of a major museum exhibition she had organized on the work of black women artists. Reluctantly Naomi offers that the answer to why she and her husband developed separate tastes is locked in their family upbringing, an unimportant difference to her as a young bride.

"Not only were we in love, but we were also very good friends," another woman reminisces. "In fact, we felt sorry for our college classmates who thought that they had to marry, because that was so untrue of us." Therefore, in her vision of the future, Marilyn Mc-Clintock never anticipated divorce, but neither did she plan to become the editor of a flourishing magazine. She keenly remembers the fear of carving out a career to support a young family and offers with sincerity: "If a couple stays married, that's wonderful. But if they don't, a woman doesn't have to lose life as she knew it. There can be new life."

Marilyn and Peter married two days after their college commencement. They were able to laugh away family tensions stimulated by the disappointment Peter's parents felt because he was marrying an Episcopalian from the University of Michigan rather than a Catholic from Manhattanville College. Immediately the newlyweds moved to Connecticut because Peter was in a training program for a New York bank. They figured that Marilyn could find a job until she became pregnant.

For two years she wrote for the house organ of a New York corporation. The same day that Marilyn was offered a raise and promotion, the gynecologist confirmed her pregnancy: "I was alone in understanding the irony; I even felt guilty about noticing it." But after their second child was born, Marilyn felt "locked in" and found part-time positions in writing and research for various national institutes and agencies. Her talents were brought to the attention of *The New Yorker*, and she was offered a position: "I had two weeks to decide, and knew I had to say no. But I didn't call until four o'clock on the second Friday."

Peter had calculated that the costs for child care, travel, and a new professional wardrobe would not balance against Marilyn's salary. Although disappointed by the choice she had to make, Marilyn had never seriously considered grooming her own career.

Within months of rejecting *The New Yorker*, Marilyn recalls that their marriage began to flounder when Peter uprooted his family to pursue an independent business venture with a partner in Seattle. The business folded and Peter lost money. More significant, Marilyn questioned his business ethics and challenged his loss of integrity. Peter found solace with another woman, but Marilyn forgave him when he returned. The second time he strayed, she lost trust and they parted.

But Marilyn's firm decision to separate did not quell her anxiety about raising two children under six years of age by herself: "I couldn't imagine life without being married. I always expected to have a wonderful husband, a nice yard, and good schools for the children.

When I would see families in station wagons, tears would roll down my face."

Besides being deeply disappointed, Marilyn was angry that she was psychologically unprepared, despite her talents, to be the breadwinner. She realized her two options: to become immobilized as a living monument to her anger or to use her anger as a motivating force. "Therefore, I rose up and declared to the world, 'By God, I will get a job on my own, and I will succeed.'"

True to her promise, Marilyn began in sales for a national magazine. Through talent and hard work, she is now an editor of a successful business magazine. "On good days, I thought I would get here; but on bad days, I wondered how I could go on. If I had it to do over again, I would have come out of my malaise much sooner than I did."

The self-destructive temptation for divorced women is to assume the role of passive victim, for then their lives become actual testimony to the wrongs that they have endured. But instead of such behavior penalizing their husbands, women restrict their own freedom by denying the fact that life can change when one exercises choice. Women who take charge of their lives after divorce admit, confront, and experience their anger without falling into the trap of seeking ways to perpetuate it. At some point they choose, as Marilyn did, between making the divorce the centerfold of their lives or blowing it off.

Divorced women who actively shape new lives for themselves resolve their future by putting disappointment and hostility behind them. They eventually assume the attitude of Virginia Woolf, the great English novelist and literary critic, who, after lamenting a disheartening visit to Oxford, finally decided that it was time "to roll up the crumpled skin of the day, with its arguments and its impressions and its anger and its laughter, and cast it into the hedges."

CHAPTER 3

Burning Doors

Divorce is like standing in the middle of a burning house, where the only exit is through a burning door. If you go through it, you know you will be scarred. But the alternative is to stay and die.

Sara McDevitt
October 10, 1987

Divorces occur for many reasons, but common to all of them is pain. Women who rebound from divorce to create satisfying lives may appear to be the lucky ones who escape unscathed. The perception may exist that, at best, their suffering was superficial or, at worst, protected by callousness. Not so.

In their struggle to establish new lives, such women have attempted suicide; others have become alcoholic. All of them have known the terror of helplessness, the grief of betrayal, the plunge into loneliness, the fight to survive. Some have even been frightened at witnessing their primitive need for revenge. "How do you ever explain emotional devastation? I felt lucky to get through the day," confides a woman who now holds an executive position.

Women who defined themselves after divorce were not immune to suffering the range of debilitating marital relationships. They were abused, raped, ridiculed, and forgotten. They were the disillusioned victims of lies. They knew the tension of disguising their talent and intelligence. They lost their husbands to other women and to younger men. But finally they triumphed from the ruins of divorce because of who they are, not because of what they have.

Seven years ago a woman who now earns more than $150,000 a year as an institutional broker in a major securities corporation attempted suicide because she was a dependent homemaker in a financially and emotionally bankrupt marriage. One Sunday afternoon, Phyllis Corbett tied a plastic bag around her head and turned on the gas. After more than an hour, awakened by a ringing telephone, she muttered from within the kitchen oven, "Oh, shit, it didn't work." Phyllis's note had read, "I just want to be good at something."

Phyllis managed residential investment properties she and her husband owned. She researched their market value, structured lease agreements, supervised work crews, and dealt with the tenants. "Yet," she says, "I thought he did it all." After they moved into a Victorian home that required extensive remodeling, Phyllis learned that Stephen had borrowed against their real estate and had forged her signature to third and fourth mortgages. Now their properties were being foreclosed.

Sitting penniless in her gutted house with two teenage children, Phyllis sold the dining room set in order to pay the plumber for a functioning bathroom. Stephen was seldom at home and cared little about the living conditions endured by his wife and children. Pursued by creditors, Phyllis declined in mental and physical health because she saw no way to change a hopeless situation. She cried constantly, stayed in bed, and survived on coffee, M&M's, and Pepsi. Then, learning about her husband's mistress and overwhelmed by not having a job, car, or money, Phyllis attempted suicide.

When a friend took her to the hospital and a psychiatrist began to make arrangements for her to be committed as a psychiatric patient, Phyllis gained her first strength: "There was absolutely no way anybody was going to lock me up! I had allowed myself to be the victim of others' choices for too long."

With twelve hundred dollars saved from consulting she had done for an interior designer, Phyllis moved from the gutted house into a modest apartment that realtor friends allowed her to have temporarily free of rent. For six months she budgeted her small savings and lived with the guilt of having left her son and daughter. "But I was so sick, so ineffectual, that I was no good to them anyway. I had to get myself together by first getting a job. In thirty-eight years I never had thought about being a breadwinner, and now I was on my own to cope with survival. I knew somehow that committing suicide, being a bag lady, or becoming a hooker were not my only options."

Phyllis worked two part-time jobs that employed her seven days a week as a salesclerk. Her motivation to succeed increased steadily, especially when her daughter came to live with her. Within a year Phyllis began to set reasonable goals for herself, even though the court had made her responsible for one-third of the marital debts. Stephen, having lost his corporate position of fifteen years, claimed bankruptcy for his share. Needing more money, Phyllis got a job in residential interior design for a furniture store but, contrary to her expectations, spent most of her time in straight sales and was soon fired because of a lackluster record. One of her former employers then promised her a permanent position as a salesclerk, but the vacancy would not occur for three months. In despair, Phyllis learned she was eligible for unemployment compensation. But, as she stood in the unemployment line, her conscience was not clear: "I was not convinced that I deserved the money, but I needed it; it was available, so I held out my hand." Phyllis faced a painful truth: "I had been marking time until a man would come along to take care of me. I knew in that line that I wanted to be master of my own destiny."

Phyllis gave herself a year to sort out career options and make conscious decisions that would affect the rest of her life. To do this, she interviewed eighty men and women, asking them probing questions about their professions and careers. She sat in her local library reading volumes of trade and business journals. Her fields of interest narrowed to the food and computer industries, but most particularly to financial services and securities, "probably because they seemed far beyond my reach. I was forty years old and did not know the difference between stocks and bonds."

Phyllis interviewed another dozen persons employed in securities, asking why she should buy from them rather than a competitor. By the end of the year, Phyllis had received four job offers to train as a retail investment broker. Close to making a decision, she was offered an even more challenging position in institutional sales, where she would be trained as a broker in a major investment firm.

Within seven years from her suicide attempt, Phyllis became vice-president for sales and marketing for one of the nation's largest bank and financial services corporations. She delights in repeating her daughter's insight: "Mom, you're like Scarlett O'Hara, determined never to be hungry again." Quickly setting her values straight, Phyllis adds, "I believe I can prosper without cheating, lying, stealing, or living with a man I don't love. The only revenge is living well."

Phyllis did not have the luxury of time to prepare for a professional career or the inclination to return to school for an advanced degree. Yet once she had emotional control, she carefully plotted a course of action and advanced up the corporate ladder with meteoric speed. Generally women in the throes of divorce are not so disciplined in defining their goals. For example, Barbara Reed is in the same income bracket as Phyllis. Within the past five years her net worth has soared to a million and a half as a real estate developer in Maine. But ten years ago she followed very simple criteria in applying for a real estate license: "I didn't want to go into a service job or be a secretary. Friends recommended that I be a caterer simply because I was a good cook. Selling real estate was the one thing I thought I could do without worrying that my mother would turn over in her grave. I also had lived in a lot of houses, and people said I would be good at it."

Barbara moved frequently because her husband, Richard, an attorney, gave up practicing in his father's New Hampshire firm to begin a new career as a prep school headmaster. After Richard finished a master's degree in education at a southern university, the Reeds began their odyssey from east to west, moving sometimes annually from school to school.

During their engagement, Barbara recognized Richard as a hard drinker, but they saw each other only on college weekends, where "everyone was drinking, so I couldn't tell if he really had a problem." Barbara and Richard were blessed with charm, intelligence, and their parents' money. "We blended very well," Barbara confides, "but my values at age twenty were shallow; in fact, now I say I married him to be a breeder. I thought Richard would be a wonderful father because he had been a great counselor at a boys' summer camp in Maine. I thought our wedding was a beautiful big party. I had no concept of the problems I would be facing."

Very soon Barbara was able to anticipate Richard's drinking pattern from bender to bender. She wanted to divorce him even before their first anniversary but didn't proceed when she knew she was pregnant.

Barbara felt isolated with her problems. Not wanting to contribute to the fragility of her mother's emotional health, she would not confide in her parents. Furthermore, she lived on Richard's turf in a prestigious New Hampshire community in an elegant home given to them by Richard's father. Resentment ran high that

Richard, the town's catch, had not married one of their own: "I had to be smart, beautiful, and perfect to show that Richard had done very well. I had to have a serene exterior, like Grace Kelly."

But when Richard decided to change careers, it was to Barbara that his father gave one hundred thousand dollars, "rather like a payoff to take care of his son and grandchildren because he knew that Richard was not in control of himself." Dutifully, Barbara followed Richard from one unsuccessful prep school stint to another. She worked in interior design studios, a respectable position for a headmaster's wife, and coped night and day with trying to hide the extent of Richard's drinking. Barbara admits to enduring this peripatetic and strained existence because she didn't know how she could ever succeed independently: "Richard managed to convince me that he was bright and I was stupid because I hadn't finished my degree. The message was deep in my psyche that I couldn't succeed. Yet I had to take care of this brilliant man as if he were the third child in our family."

Barbara continued to protect him even after they left the prep school world to live in Maine, the place of happy childhood memories where Richard thought he could restore himself by practicing law. While Richard studied for the bar exam, Barbara surreptitiously read his books to prepare for a real estate license. The move to Maine only aggravated Richard's drinking, however. His law practice a shambles, Barbara once again offered protection as his legal secretary. She also worked short hours at a real estate office where she was not permitted floor time to answer the telephone. Within a short time, Barbara and Richard had no money.

But when Richard's mother died and left him a bequest, Barbara borrowed against it to buy a small house, which she used as a real estate office. The inheritance was quickly spent trying to rehabilitate Richard at detoxification hospitals. After each hospitalization, Richard would return to his previous behavior. Barbara knew she had to leave, "but I just could not break free of the role of caretaker. I needed backbone, emotional strength, and the promise of money to support the children. I had done everything humanly possible for Richard, so that I would never feel guilty. But for my own salvation, we had to divorce. I had to realize that I wasn't God. If I wanted to martyr myself, I couldn't sacrifice the children. We craved peace."

In the divorce settlement, Barbara wanted only their house: "Alimony or a lump settlement was out of the question because you can't get blood from a stone. Besides that, when I feel poor, I push hardest."

Barbara Reed is now owner and president of one of Portland's most prosperous real estate companies, with branch offices employing over twenty brokers. "When I opened my first little office ten years ago, I didn't even consider the risks. I just knew I had to do something fast. There was no money; the children had to be fed and the mortgage had to be paid." Barbara is not cynical about her long journey to achieve peace and success: "If Richard Reed had not had a drinking problem, I'd probably be lounging at the country club now. I would never have explored or known my potential. But it is too bad that I had to discover it because of human waste."

If Barbara Reed had finished her bachelor's degree, she would have had more confidence in her resources to support herself and her children. But a college education and an enviable employment record will not minimize the threat of an unknown future for a divorced woman who has always valued her own career as secondary to her husband's.

To change from a job to career mentality, Emily Schaub had to shift her entire perspective. Now she is vice-president of sales and marketing for a leading corporation in the computer industry, earning, with bonuses, $150,000 annually. But shortly after her marriage, she traded Capitol Hill for the Junior League. Emily, a press secretary for a U.S. congressman and then a senator, worked on the 1968 presidential campaign in California when Robert Kennedy was assassinated. After marrying Ken Schaub, whom she had dated sporadically for five years, she moved with him to a midwestern city where he was a market analyst for a corporation. Emily clearly defined her options: complain about missing the excitement of Capitol Hill or become an active volunteer in civic organizations.

The president of the board of the city symphony, quickly spotting her talents in publications for the Junior League and art museum, offered her a position as public relations director. Then the mayor of the city doubled her salary to manage publicity for his reelection campaign. From the time she left Washington, Emily had never stopped working, even when her children were infants. Yet she makes a distinction between holding interesting jobs and pursuing a satisfying career. When Kenneth was transferred to national headquarters in Chicago, she became an assistant director of corporate communications for one of the city's largest banks, a position she loved and which promised a future. But within three years another transfer for Kenneth took them full cycle, back to Washington, D.C.

Emily stayed behind in Chicago, working at her job and attending to all of the duties of the corporate wife: selling the house, buying a new house, and waiting for the children to finish school. "It never occurred to me to do things differently," Emily says, "to be less than Supermom. I had given up all of my jobs to follow Ken without any question about whose future might be brighter."

Emily continued working in Washington as a development director for a national funding agency but quit because a demanding travel schedule drew her away from home. "Professionally, I would be described as assertive, a leader, but within my marriage," Emily reveals, "I was ultimately dependent upon Ken for all decisions. He supported me in everything I wanted to do. We were really best friends, I thought. He was totally involved with me and the girls. We decorated the house and chose our china together; he bought me clothes and jewelry. He even told me what earrings to wear in the morning. He was an excellent father; in fact, I made a conscious decision not to breast-feed the girls so that he could also have the experience of nursing them."

Consequently, when Ken told her that he was leaving her for another woman, Emily was more devastated than one who knew only the public Emily might have expected her to be. "The day he left," Emily says, laughing, "I cried to a friend over a bag lunch in Lafayette Square that I had no idea who would cut the girls' toenails! That tells you about my dependency."

While Emily was trying to deal with her feelings of deep, personal betrayal, she also was facing betrayal at work. She was not able to acknowledge her divorce because she was the only woman administrator in an office of chauvinistic men, waiting for her first mistake. "When I would pass by, one of the vice-presidents would mutter, 'Broads are only good in bedrooms or kitchens.'" Then she discovered that her boss had tapped her telephone, listening in on intimate conversations between Emily and her lawyer, physician, and priest. Emily shakes her head: "I was so dependent upon my ex-husband as my confidant that I even grieved more because, ironically, I thought he was the only one who could understand my feelings now. Yet I lacked self-worth because he had left me."

Emily was also living from paycheck to paycheck, often having less than five dollars at the end of the month. Legal fees and the move to Washington had wiped out her savings. Determined that nothing would change the life of her daughters, Emily decided that her only option was to pursue a career, not just interesting jobs: "I didn't want to have to remarry in order to maintain our life-style or function as a family." This clarity came to her one Sunday morning when the girls proposed that they take a fifty-mile bike hike. Before Ken had left, the four of them would ride in a line with the girls between their parents. Emily answered spontaneously, "We can't do that. Who would ride in front and back?" No sooner were the words out of her mouth than she realized how such an attitude could permanently cripple her daughters' lives. "I decided then that I could be anything I wanted to be, and the three of us could be a family. We took our bike ride. You only need a fourth for bridge."

Emily involved the children in all of her career decisions, including relocating to a major midwestern city. The girls agreed that if they were not willing to compromise the standard of living that they had enjoyed before the divorce, "then they had to give up their expectations that I would always be available." Emily's teenage daughters take pride in their mother's career and their family solidarity. Emotionally Emily thought she had recovered from the divorce at the end of a year; now she knows it really took four years before "my highs were not as high and my lows were not as low." Again, she was aware of the distance between her private feelings and public image.

The financial independence that women seek after divorce equates money with autonomy, ego, freedom, and independence, not merely with the acquisition of goods. Money is not the ultimate benchmark by which they measure self-worth and success. Equally important are personal growth and inner peace. An attorney who began law school after her divorce twelve years ago clarifies her values: "Certainly I'm financially secure, but I needed to be successful just for me; to say that I had accomplished something on my own." It is the rare woman who will not say, "I never want to have to ask a man for money again." This view, however, is not to be equated with a fiercely competitive spirit.

Jessica Schumann, for example, knew she needed money before she could set herself free to write. Not unlike Ibsen's Hedda Gabler, Jessica married because she had danced herself tired and her father had decided that it was time. She perceived her husband as a glamorous and intellectual caretaker, but his conversation wore thin when she had to be quiet about her own achievements.

Jessica, who has a master's degree in creative writing, worked as a technical writer before marrying Theodore Schumann, a brilliant young physicist who patented his discoveries, lectured in European universities, consulted for major corporations, and won grants from prestigious foundations. Jessica quit working, had three children, and traveled with her famous husband as he won more recognition. Meanwhile, she stopped writing. After five years of silence, she began a short story that took her seven years to complete. When at last she gave it proudly to Theodore to read, he commented, "What is this women's stuff you're writing?" Jessica never showed him another line.

For six more years she continued acting as Theodore's hostess, frequently giving parties for over one hundred persons, entertaining packs of graduate students, and serving Theodore breakfast in bed. She carried out his insistent demands to clean the cellar, straighten the medicine cabinet, and brew quantities of herbal tea simply because she could not bear to listen to his loquacious diatribes whenever he was thwarted. "To survive," she says, "one must do what one must." One morning, as she listened to the private rehearsal of a chamber music quartet, Jessica suddenly thought, I can't make beautiful music, but I can make beautiful words and must not be afraid to let out what is inside me.

Each morning after that moment of illumination, Jessica was up at five o'clock writing in her journal because "after so many years I had to learn my craft." Jessica's self-analysis required four more years, but she emerged as a published writer, often called upon to teach writing courses and conduct workshops on college campuses. She had prepared to leave Theodore step by step. She could not continue living with a man who refused to respect her talent, but neither could she continue to write separated from him without the financial security to make it on her own. Jessica slammed the door on twenty-two years of marriage only when she was able to buy a small house for herself on the Maine coast, a place that had always fed her soul. "I have enough to live simply and to write. I would scrub floors in a surgical ward rather than go back to my former life."

After making up her mind to leave him, years, in fact, before actually doing so, Jessica was able to drain off her tension by accepting Theodore as a person with incredible foibles, rather than as the romantic husband who had not fulfilled his promise. She minimized her suffering by letting the marriage go long before the official separation.

Most women do not plan their moment of separation as consciously and furtively as Jessica Schumann. Isabel Howell was on automatic pilot. Different from Theodore Schumann, John Howell did encourage his wife's creativity, probably because he liked the idea of " 'my wife, the artist,' " comments Isabel. But his approval did not inspire Isabel to paint. She absorbed so much petty criticism about unironed polo shirts and unimaginative dinners that her energies were drained. Furthermore, John would punish her by withdrawing sex: "I spent most of my time trying to figure out what was wrong with me, trying to please him."

Suspecting John's philandering for years, Isabel "followed the fucker" one spring evening, a month before she had arranged for her first exhibit to be hung in a small gallery. Only now does Isabel understand that her decision to confront John and file for divorce was based on the glimmer that she could possibly support herself as an artist. Balancing her risks and gains, Isabel, who had strong fears about living independently, now says simply, "I gained my mental health. I no longer had to be in bed with John talking forever and ever. It was like being married to *Time* magazine. I'm myself now. My goal is to have a Manhattan exhibit within five years. But no matter what, divorce is still very sad; it's the breakup of a family."

On the day her divorce was granted, Alice Crouch was also sad. Weary that her settlement had taken so long, she expected to be jubilant on her last day in court. "But when the judge said the divorce was granted, I felt a terribly deep sorrow because I had married Jim when I was eighteen, and now I was forty."

Alice, an only child, was only four years old when her mother died at age thirty-eight. After living a few years with her alcoholic father, she was appointed by the court to make her home with an aunt. Alice and Jim were high school sweethearts: "Jim was everything to me: husband, brother, and father. Except for the past few years, our life had been wonderful."

Alice had been willing to forgive her husband's infidelity as a midlife crisis. "Jim's affairs didn't break up our marriage," she analyzes. "We had too much of a history together which I treasured. I could deal with Jim's having a fling and sleeping with somebody. But it was his effort to put me on the defensive in order to rationalize his behavior that caused the real pain. He would pick fights over nothing; berate me for cooking a pork roast instead of a London broil; then he would feel justified for going off with Suzy-Q for the weekend."

Alice accepted Jim back time and time again. One marriage counselor, after a few sessions with Alice, advised that she stop wasting money and see an attorney. Still Alice persisted in believing that Jim would reform. During one separation, she questioned her own behavior when Jim didn't come home for a dinner that he had begged her to prepare so that they could talk one more time. Two days later when Jim did appear, the dinner was still on the table. In front of him, Alice threw the dishes and all of the pots and pans into the garbage can. "That was the only way I had to make my point," she says with dismay. "But Jim just had me crazy with his erratic behavior."

The last chance she gave him was to grant his appeal to join her and their teenage daughter for Thanksgiving dinner at a hotel in their southern city. Their attempt to look like a model family was short-lived, however, when the dining room reminded Jim to share stories about times he had enjoyed there with his latest girlfriend. Alice began to hyperventilate and was rushed by ambulance to a nearby hospital. Now thirty-eight years old, she was scared because both her mother and her father's mother had died at the same age. Finally she saw an attorney.

Alice filed for divorce, uncertain about her future. Whatever her financial risk, she could not continue living in a relationship so debilitating to her and threatening to her daughter. She began a conscious struggle for independence by examining with new eyes her volunteer experience in the city where she had lived during her entire married life. Alice gradually realized that for many years she had absorbed Jim's trivialization of her civic involvement, thus minimizing her accomplishments as coordinator of the Junior League Thrift Shop and as chairperson for a citywide high school art exhibit.

Alice also felt satisfaction at solving the riddle of Jim's behavior: "Until I deliberately evaluated my life, I hadn't realized that I had started to grow and was no longer the insecure eighteen-year-old that Jim had married. If I would tell him I had been offered a job because someone admired the work I was doing for the league, he would say, 'Oh, honey, if you do that, you won't be able to paper the bathroom,' or, 'That would keep us back from going on vacation.' And I'd just say, 'Okay.' I guess he needed to have someone more dependent upon him than I, so he turned to younger women."

Newly divorced, Alice is capitalizing on the skills she learned as a volunteer. She is a representative for a popular cosmetic firm, selling to major department stores. She has given herself a year to gain confidence and sort out her future. "It's tempting," she confides, "to look for a man to take care of me, but I enjoy the feeling of making my own decisions and having my own money. And if I do remarry, I'll never go back to scratch where I have nothing in my own right. Even if I win millions of dollars in the lottery, I'll keep working."

Alice did not lose self-esteem because of Jim's affairs with other women. She was always willing to forgive him one more time, because their long and happy marriage measured more to her than his short-term affairs. Wives who lose their husbands to younger men instead of younger women do not have the solace, however, of making distinctions between marital history and midlife flings.

One of these women, a certified public accountant in a major firm, after her divorce climbed to ranks seldom achieved by a woman. "But," she confesses, "I had no self-worth at all, even though I was achieving professionally." Her only relief was in finally knowing why she never quite pleased her husband. "I would think, if I let my hair grow, he will like me better. If I cut my hair short, he will like me better. Maybe if I learn to ski or improve my tennis. It's terrible to be in bed and be constantly rejected. It's devastating to be replaced by a man."

In time, this woman restored herself to complete psychic health while simultaneously advancing in her career. She recalls a Saturday morning when her young son and daughter left for skating lessons and she returned to bed to cry. Very soon she remembered that the next day was Easter and if she didn't get to the candy store, the children would not have baskets. This urgency not to miss the fleeting pleasures of life inevitably strengthened her. "Now," she marvels, "it's even hard to imagine that I once wondered how I would get dressed to face the day."

True freedom for divorced women who express pride in their accomplishments means active participation in the experiences of life. They choose their lives and take responsibility for their decisions. "God didn't put anyone here with the explicit task of making me happy or paying my way," remarks a woman who for twenty years conformed to her husband's idea of what a wife should be. "I came to understand that only I can really set the tone for my day; only I can stop myself from being miserable. I'm the one who finally has to get on with it." Sometimes the lives these women choose for themselves are even counter to new stereotypic expectations for the successful, independent woman.

Eileen Rossi, age forty, has said no, for example, to an opportunity to double her annual salary of fifty thousand dollars because she does not want to be on the fast track within corporate management. Presently the manager of an employment agency that is part of a national chain, Eileen rejected an offer to join the national office and train for a top management position. The rewards of competition would not substitute for the time and space she now enjoys. A bout with cancer influenced her priorities.

Eileen was married for ten years when her breast cancer was diagnosed at age thirty-six. Within that same year she closed her eyes to suspicions that her husband was "fooling around." Always having worked at part-time positions in sales, Eileen was never on a career path, even though her salary was important to the family budget.

On the day of the biopsy, Matt dropped Eileen off at the hospital but didn't stay. She could barely speak when she called him with the results. To the physician's explanation about surgical options for breast cancer, Matt responded: "Does this mean she can't have any more babies?" "Not would I live or die," Eileen interprets.

After her mastectomy, Eileen had radiation therapy every day for six weeks. Not once did Matt drive her to the hospital; the neighbors arranged a carpool. Physically and emotionally drained, Eileen spent most of the six weeks in bed. After a month Matt wondered why she didn't secure another job: "People who have triple bypass surgery are back at work sooner than you," he said. Eileen's parents were aghast at Matt's lack of compassion.

When confronted by Eileen about his seeing another woman, Matt insisted that her imagination was working overtime. But credit card receipts and motel bills were left carelessly on his dresser. Eileen figured out where his girlfriend lived and paid them a visit one night. Weak from surgery and radiation, she nevertheless bounded up the stairs, past the nymphet who opened the door, and accosted Matt, standing nude in the bathroom.

"I felt such rage," Eileen remembers, "that I knew how a person could commit murder." But it was Matt who spent the next months in rancor. Eileen remained at home with their teenage daughter, but they were without a car or heat. Matt was in the plumbing business, but when the furnace broke Eileen had to borrow money to have it repaired. And one day when she was at the hospital, Matt took the television set and electrical appliances. Eileen's parents gave her five hundred dollars to see an attorney.

"I was so shocked at realizing that if I had had a gun, I would have shot Matt in that bathroom," Eileen whispers, "that I made up my mind that my revenge would be in outstripping his salary within five years." But she did it within three years by increasing her earnings from eighteen thousand dollars in 1984 to fifty thousand in 1987. But Eileen chose not to accept a promotion to join company headquarters or to vie for similar high-powered positions because she did not want "to eat, sleep, and drink my work." She is happy with the quality of her life and needs nothing more. Nightmares about the past still interrupt Eileen's sleep, but each morning she looks toward the light and welcomes the day. Most of all, she wants to stay healthy in order to help her daughter, a college senior, graduate from law school.

The raw insight that one must die by herself made Eileen Rossi aware that she must also live for herself. With similar vision, women who triumph from divorce know that life will slip through their fingers if they hold on to memories of pain. By letting go of hostility, grief, and revenge, they gain power to control their destinies and, furthermore, to enjoy their lives. In fact, women who escape turbulent marriages do not necessarily want to erase those years. Although many admit that they should have delayed marriage until defining themselves better, they quickly cite, almost in the same breath, the children they would not have. If it is possible to make the distinction, these women would not rewrite their lives without the marriage, because to do so betrays the children whom they love. Moreover, they are proud and confident of the identities that they have shaped from the ashes of divorce.

Elizabeth Hampsey, a suburban matron who gave up a country club existence to attend law school by living on welfare, food stamps, and minimum wage jobs, would not sacrifice one bit of her suffering. "Without it, I would not have ended up where I did," she claims. "Existentially, I would not have what I have. You sort of bump into trees if you like where you are now. I would not change one iota of my life because I adore my kids and practicing law. Had I gone to law school in the early sixties, I doubt I would have had the stamina to put up with what women did then. I probably would have quit, married, and wandered off into some suburban traffic jam."

A similar response is offered by writer Jessica Schumann: "Certainly I should have left after two weeks, except I had to do what I did to get where I am now. I know what life is about, and because of that knowledge I have no regrets."

Elizabeth and Jessica express the confidence of other women who rejoice in the freedom of knowing who they are. They emerge from divorce on the far side of despair, finding hope in the new persons they have become. Their way beyond crisis has not been around it, but through the burning door, "bumping into trees," starting the new journey.

CHAPTER 4

New Beginnings

I was a rag doll in the corner and the world was passing me by. I was screaming for help and no one could hear me. Then I thought, Just stand up and walk with them.

Lorraine Lucas
October 30, 1987

Women who direct their own destinies after divorce respond actively to domestic crisis, even if temporarily incapacitated by pain, suffering, and grief. They do not passively allow the drama of their lives to play itself out, accepting and relishing the role of victimized woman. Indeed, their cycle of renewal often begins when they are experiencing intense anger, anxiety, despair, or loneliness. In these unlikely situations, their consciousness first stirs that it is within their power to begin again. Even in the darkest hour of marriage, a woman will discover strength for self-definition.

Women who affirm themselves through divorce also seek emotional support from a variety of sources that suit their personal style and needs. They attend workshops and lectures that address issues of divorce. With new eyes they read the works of women writers or explore the lives of women characters in fiction. They value professional counseling from psychologists or psychiatrists. With open arms they welcome the neighbor who arrives at the kitchen door bearing two martinis in a soup kettle. But whatever support they choose, women who truly want to make it on their own after divorce neither await the arrival of a savior nor lounge in a state of sentimental malaise.

Joanne Hennigan describes the lowest point in her marriage as, paradoxically, the first time that she experienced the dawn of possible new meaning. She remembers the incident that poisoned the last vestiges of her love.

After a short career as a registered nurse, Joanne worked solely as a homemaker. "When I got married, I wanted a family to be my career. I wanted to be another Ethel Kennedy, minus the fortune." For ten years she tried to fulfill her dream by denying her husband's drinking problem. Finally confronting Dennis that she intended to see a marriage counselor because their family life was becoming intolerable, he responded with venom: "I've got you where the hairs are short. You can't go anywhere." Numbed by such hatefulness, Joanne felt the death of all mutual trust and respect. But she also felt the stirrings of a new determination. Determined that she would no longer wait up at night for Dennis to return from his carousing, she enjoyed a sense of freedom. Without planning for a future that she could really name, she nonetheless enrolled in college courses.

For another few years Dennis maintained his position in corporate management. Hiding flasks of Manhattans

72

in his baseball mitt, he even tried to be a good father by coaching Little League games. But his physical and emotional deterioration continued to the point where he experienced delirium tremens. Through it all, Joanne cooperated with every effort of physicians to rehabilitate him. She gave up only when he tried to kill both of them while driving their car one ordinary afternoon to the supermarket. As a result, friends begged her to leave Dennis. Even his boss advised: "If this man doesn't start to improve, then I think you should separate and let him go."

But Joanne felt too helpless and insecure to act. It was only in absolute desperation, after Dennis had drunk himself into a suicidal stupor and lay on the living room floor in front of the children's friends, that Joanne admitted him to a veterans hospital. Then she took the first step toward her own renewal: she accepted the offer of an old family friend to arrange a job as an executive secretary, a step that also meant she had to move from her home in upstate New York to Philadelphia.

"It was not simply a matter of leaving Dennis," Joanne explains. "I was scared about defining myself as separate from him. I just had to keep telling myself that 'no matter what else is out there, it can't be as bad as what you've been through.' So I kept walking, straight ahead, trusting in my friends, knowing that I somehow had to make a better life for my children." Joanne's immediate goal, in fact, was simply to live through the job interview. But she surprised even herself by her facility in answering questions: "At least I began to have some assurance that I wouldn't end up with a can of beer in front of the TV for the rest of my life."

During the last few days she lived in her Syracuse home, Joanne kept, underneath her pillow, a picture of her new Philadelphia apartment, which friends also had selected. Sometimes trembling with fear, she held that picture as if it were a talisman: "Just looking at it made me understand that I had chosen a life of my own and no one would be drunk there."

Although cramped in a small apartment with young children, Joanne had space for private reflection and realized it was "all right to think my own thoughts. My whole life had been built on my marriage, no matter how horrible it was. I felt as if a limb had been cut off. I felt as though I were a wounded butterfly, dragging along the ground, managing and managing. It's a real loss to end a marriage."

On the other hand, Joanne had courage to pray at night: " 'Please, dear God, do not send anyone to save me. I want to manage on my own.' I knew that if some nice man came along, I would say, 'I've had enough.' I remember the night I finally was able to say, 'All right, God. You can go ahead now.' "

Joanne credits the feminist movement for rebuilding her self-confidence, particularly *The Feminine Mystique*. "Oh, I was silly for a while and went two months without wearing a bra. But reading and discussing *The Feminine Mystique* with other women, even in the best years of our marriage, helped me to find courage when I needed it." By herself in a new city, Joanne depended upon her reading for emotional support: "I drew strength from feminism because I felt so used and worthless. I needed every bit of affirmation I could get, and I knew it was up to me to look for it."

Joanne also accepted help from a remarkable woman, one of the first in corporate management, who had no trace of the "queen bee syndrome" that once defined the personalities of so many women who had succeeded in a male world. When Joanne began working in the corporation, this vice-president gave her five hundred dollars and said: "I know how difficult things must be for you now, but you'll make it."

To this day Joanne tries to continue the legacy of her benefactor by "putting my money where my mouth is." If not money, she offers support that breeds self-reliance, not self-pity: "A heartsick woman will not develop independence by hearing someone commiserate, 'Oh, you poor thing.' There are better ways to help her."

Within a few years Joanne Hennigan took another risk: she applied for the position of ombudsman for a model community in Virginia. She is still proud of how she answered the developer who expressed concern that "you don't have a husband, and people will take advantage of that." Joanne relieved him of his worry by noting, "In a single-parent household, family life is restructured and individuals have different responsibilities." Her forthrightness helped her to get the job, even though she had no prior experience in real estate development.

Eventually Joanne returned to the medical profession, earning over thirty-five thousand dollars a year as the administrative head of a medical unit of a university hospital. She remarried at forty-eight and after a few years quit her position to finish her bachelor's degree: "I thrived on the recognition I received by organizing an office with six physicians and a large support staff. But I know I'm doing what I'm supposed to be doing. Kids in my classes complain about assignments or reading being a waste of time. But I never feel that way. At fifty-two, I'm finally spending time on me!"

Women in disintegrating marriages will often sense their freedom when they feel most lost. Somehow in this desperate state, they will plumb resources they did not know they had and timidly begin to control their destiny. Even when they feel trapped without any clear horizon, women like Joanne Hennigan will tentatively set their course on a different tack, following faint winds that hint of better ways to live.

Like Joanne Hennigan, Lorraine Lucas also remembers the lowest point in her marriage as the time when she first had intimations of her own strength. She describes being in a state of emotional paralysis, where she sat for days like a "rag doll in the corner and the world was passing me by. I was screaming for help and no one could hear me. Then I thought, Just stand up and walk with them."

A mother with four children under ten years of age, Lorraine hungered for some life of the mind, a need her husband belittled. She would vacuum the rug and think, I was a chemistry major, and now I only sweep. When Lorraine enrolled in a course at the community college, Ted embarrassed her in front of friends by saying: "Oh, she thinks she's so smart going to college." But he flexed his final control over her by violently disrupting her studying and then, on at least three occasions, raping her. "I felt dead after the first experience," Lorraine confides. "Even now, I don't seem to have the words to talk about it."

They tried one last attempt to understand each other by attending a church-sponsored marriage-encounter weekend. Their previous efforts to communicate openly were short-circuited because "Ted would always throw everything back at me the next time he got pissed." But Lorraine wanted to save their marriage because she truly valued it as a deep sacramental commitment.

During the encounter weekend, "Ted glowed with love for me," Lorraine continues. "And he thought I glowed, too, but I died. He was thrilled and I was suffering. I knew I didn't want to be in love with him." Lorraine was filled with anguish because she was admitting that their marriage was not a sacramental exchange where she and Ted gave life and love to each other. Ted, on the other hand, high from the romance of incense, enkindled his own dream. As the protective prince, he would carry his bride to their split-level palace and ensconce her forever in a La-Z-Boy recliner. Consequently Lorraine went home and sat it out for a week.

But, as an only child, Lorraine was very practiced in sitting alone and thinking. She knew that her salvation depended upon her ability to resist surrendering to Ted's definition of a holy marriage. She says simply, "I believed in the goodness of who I was as a person. It was sinful for me to be trapped anymore. No one could help me but myself. There was no use trying to scream. So I stood up and showered."

It was Ted who filed for divorce, however. He could not see himself living with the person that Lorraine wanted to become. Contrary to his expectations, the marriage-encounter weekend had not "fixed her up." Consequently Lorraine struggled through very difficult financial years with her children before completing her doctorate and beginning a career in the field of psychology.

In recalling the lowest points of their marriages, divorced women continually depend upon words such as "suffocated," "smothered," or "stifled" to describe their feelings of helplessness. But it is often in this darkened state of mind that a woman will clearly focus on the quality of her life and, for the first time, see her own promise. Problems are not resolved at this stage, but for the awakened woman nothing will ever be the same. She will begin to act, even if the first indication of her new behavior is only in Lorraine Lucas's simple gesture of lifting herself out of a chair.

Literally a prisoner in her own home, Karen Sherman also came to know herself in very lonely circumstances. Now she is philosophical about her experience: "Sometimes a person has to sink to the bottom to face reality; if she can't build from that moment by herself, then she needs to get professional help."

The mother of a two-year-old daughter, Karen could not even leave her house to buy groceries. For two weeks she sat on a rocking chair that went nowhere.

This cycle of despondency lifted, however, when she identified her symptoms as those diagnosed as agoraphobia on a television talk show she was watching. Immediately she began to defy the state she now could name by walking to the corner grocery store to haul home storage cartons.

Karen began packing everything from baby clothes to crystal in order to leave Baltimore with her daughter and return to her parents' retirement home in North Carolina. Walking into this fury of activity, Karen's husband, Jerry, noted, "I'm glad that you're finally cleaning the house. That's the most productive thing I've seen you do in days." Karen was careful to divide their possessions in half, but Jerry did not know he was witnessing an exodus. Karen was frightened as she packed: "I was moving forward, but I didn't really know where."

Karen lit out for new territory because "the only way I could get on with my life was to get away. Yet even when I thought about suicide, somehow I knew I was crazy. My major motivation for survival was not to let my child down, but I really didn't know what I would do."

Karen had been a prisoner in her home long before she settled onto her rocking chair. She had left college after a year to marry Jerry, a sales representative for a carpet company. One month after the wedding, she knew she had made a mistake and heard echoes of her parents' words that Jerry was not the one for her. But Karen grew adept at creating happy moments with Jerry by curbing any independent thoughts or opinions on the most simple issues.

Karen worked as a dental assistant but had no access to any bank accounts or even to her own salary; she endorsed her paychecks to Jerry. She had to ask him for money to buy even the most basic items, like panty hose. She stashed away money sent to her and the baby for special occasions by her parents and eventually used it as the gift to end her marriage.

Karen wonders at the person she once was: "Six years after our divorce I look upon my marriage as something that happened to another person. I was reduced to being a slave, particularly after Molly was born because Jerry excused himself from any involvement with our lives, except to criticize." Karen estimates that she gave 150 percent trying to build a happy marriage to make up for Jerry's lack of effort: "I still thought I was being tested and could have a fairy-tale ending if I just could learn to try harder. I thought by being compliant and sweet, Jerry would come around. But instead he saw me as being weak and bullied me even more."

Trying harder for Karen meant putting down a novel when Jerry said the ironing was waiting. Trying harder meant squelching any curiosity about their bank accounts and then waiting to be doled out money. Trying harder meant ignoring the fact that Jerry spent his evenings at home behind a closed door, preoccupied with desk work.

But as Molly became a toddler and Jerry grew intolerant of her jelly-stained fingers and spilled glasses of milk, Karen recognized that she might choose to martyr herself, but not her daughter. Whatever the future, she and Molly had to leave for new territory. Karen left in August; Jerry never called her parents' home until late October. With student loans, Karen started college classes that September. Graduating with high honor, she was accepted into law school and has now been practicing for a year.

Karen's first year away from Jerry was a formative one, particularly after hiring a woman attorney to represent her. Complaining about the divorce process, Karen provoked her attorney to answer: "If you don't like the system, do something about it, but don't whine." That's when Karen began thinking about applying to law school. In an attempt to understand her own choices better, she also read books pertinent to the lives women lead: "I had to read things like *The Cinderella Complex* in order to feel strong. I had to keep telling myself that I was responsible for choosing whether or not I would be successful." Karen laughs about influencing Molly with the same message: "I indoctrinate her with dolls. The dolls marry, but they are also lawyers, doctors, writers, greengrocers, painters, and plumbers. I don't really care what Molly does, but she has to know early that life is choice; that there is no Prince Charming ready to provide."

Even though Karen Sherman and Lorraine Lucas desperately wanted to break loose from debilitating marriages, and are now on their way to building satisfying careers, they still experienced lingering feelings of grief that their marriages had failed. To leave even a disastrous marriage is to know the primal mysteries of sorrow. Initiation into the ambivalent emotions of divorce occurs, in fact, at the very moment the decision is made.

When Sara and Paul McDevitt agreed to divorce, Sara immediately removed her wedding ring but was overwhelmed by fear of the future. She explains, "On a deep psychological level I had experienced the death of my old self, but not the birth of the new. Yet regardless of risk I knew I had to walk through the burning door."

Sara, an emergency room nurse in a psychiatric hospital, met Paul when he was a college student working there as a security guard. Their families approved when they fell in love and married. Sara maintained the household until Paul graduated and also completed a master's degree in business administration. Yet Sara cannot recall one happy year that they had together. After Paul began a career as a stockbroker, it was Sara's turn to start college as a part-time student. She enrolled as an English major because it had always been her dream to be a writer. A nursing career had seemed more reasonable to her parents, who did not believe in higher education for a young woman. In some ways Paul's thinking was not much different.

As a college student, Sara experienced personal affirmation for the first time in her life. Students and faculty responded to her: "They complimented my ideas and also the way I looked." Until then Sara was not secure about herself because "Paul never seemed to like me. He never complimented me. I always felt belittled and rejected." To bolster her self-esteem, Sara frequently sought professional counseling. But on a college campus she was among people who did not simply tolerate her, as Paul did, but valued her creativity and intellectual honesty. Novels like Chopin's *The Awakening* and Flaubert's *Madame Bovary* also verified the conflicts that were real to her own life. "I was relieved by these books," Sara recalls, sighing, "to know that I wasn't crazy for having the feelings that I did. I had spent my life trying to please Paul by actually distorting who I really was."

Sara continued to try to save her marriage, however, because "I believe in marriage as an institution." She really did not want to disrupt her family life or hurt Paul. When they saw a marriage counselor together, Sara shared everything, but Paul, recalcitrant, offered nothing. Under the guise of a commuter marriage, they separated. But they reunited for a final year before deciding to divorce. Sara describes it "as the only good year of our marriage, probably because I had no real expectations, and I disassociated myself emotionally. Consequently, there were no conflicts. Also we didn't have sex, so I didn't feel compromised."

Sara and Paul divorced after moving to a northern city where Sara could begin a master of fine arts program in playwriting and their young family would not have to be separated. Sara and Paul have shared custody of their three children. The irony makes her sad: "The best part of our marriage was our family cohesiveness, not our closeness as a couple. To see my kids together only once a week is a tremendous loss." Sara treasures the family dinners that they still have with Paul for holidays and birthdays. As an only child of divorced parents, she craved strong family ties. In marriage, the family was all that she had and, ironically, what she had to give up.

The course of Sara's life was profoundly affected by her delayed education in the liberal arts. Her cycle of personal renewal began when her reading of fiction shed light on the complexities of her own experiences. Like other women who divorce, she sometimes thinks she should have ended her marriage sooner, but then stops to say: "But I like where I am now. I had to go through what I did in order to get where I am. I have to be vulnerable to be effective as a playwright. It's a price I have to pay, yet I couldn't stay open and also married to Paul."

Sara moved from a state of low self-esteem to self-acceptance by acting on the ideas, thoughts, and feelings that she had kept secret as part of her inner life. Only with great psychic strain could she have continued to keep her two worlds separate, pretending to Paul, for example, that her inner life did not exist. Sara knows that she faces a risky future as a playwright, even though her works have been performed for university audiences. She holds body and soul together with part-time teaching positions. But financial achievement is not her measure of success. She has peace in knowing, accepting, and expressing who she is.

The venture into a new state of self-awareness can stir very quietly in a woman's consciousness. Years of silent nurturing may occur before she discovers herself as separate from her various roles. Her first intuition that prescribed feminine behavior can delay or damage the expression of her individual talent may even be confusing. But it is personal circumstance, not philosophical musing, that will jar a married woman into facing the constraints in her life.

Observing the daily routine of her mother, who washed and cooked for eight children while "locked in a wretched marriage," Stephanie Vogel remembers her first troubling insight at age fourteen that women lived to serve others. But at twenty, because she was pregnant and maybe in love, Stephanie gave up a fellowship to graduate school and married. At forty-three she divorced. After the divorce she experienced a surge of euphoria but hibernated for two years trying to put her experiences into perspective. She channeled her creative energy, once drained by a troubled marriage, into organizing workshops for women on topics related to self-esteem, a project she was qualified to direct because of an earned master's degree in psychological counseling. Ironically, Stephanie attributes her listening ability as a counselor to the passive role she assumed as her husband's rapt audience: "He pontificated and I listened and asked questions. Sometimes he would say that I never talked about what I was reading; and certainly I should assume some responsibility for not taking my turn, but I just didn't have enough confidence."

Larry, a metallurgist, commuted to his Boston office from the North Shore and returned late in the evening or stayed in the city. On weekends he played golf or sailed and allowed the lion's share of child care to Stephanie, who felt lonely and unfulfilled. But she did not trust that her needs were legitimate until after reading Germaine Greer's *The Female Eunuch*, a book she credits with changing her life. She also turned to writers like George Eliot, Virginia Woolf, and Edith Wharton to seek identification with other females as portrayed by the fictional women in their novels.

Motivated by her reading, Stephanie joined a consciousness-raising group and soon confronted Larry about the emptiness she felt. So, with his support, she gradually became involved with community organizations. She was particularly drawn to committees addressing nuclear waste, air pollution, and environmental conservation. A former editor of her college newspaper, Stephanie began to cover these issues for the local press. Within a short time her work began to appear in Boston publications. But as Stephanie's reputation flourished as a free-lance writer, tension doubled at home because Larry remained detached and disinterested in her achievements. His reading material never included Stephanie's articles.

For the next twelve years Stephanie and Larry tried to help their marriage through counseling, confrontation, and even brief separations. But just as *The Female Eunuch* had earlier changed the direction of Stephanie's life, now she and Larry were profoundly affected by the slow death of a good friend.

"How much longer," Stephanie asked Larry, "should we live in tension and conflict when life is so short?" For Stephanie, the answer was a moral choice: remain married to Larry and continue denying the goodness of her own developing identity or divorce him and renege on the commitment of her wedding vows. She concluded that she could no longer define her own destiny according to the needs of another, even if it were her husband.

"But the decision was not dramatic," Stephanie concludes. "We were both burnt out and tired from years of heartache." After Larry left, Stephanie enjoyed simple pleasures like decorating a room of her own where she could read and write, surrounded by art work that she herself had chosen. "It was like nesting," Stephanie explains. "But I didn't make any changes in the family area of the house because I didn't want to add to the disruption of the children's lives, even though they were teenagers."

Stephanie no longer endures the vague sense of sadness that once permeated her life and that married women in her self-esteem workshops frequently try to describe in their counseling sessions. But because she once had the same feelings, Stephanie knows exactly what they mean.

Stephanie Vogel exemplifies women whose private sense of themselves is very fragile even though their talents are recognized publicly. For years she interpreted her husband's disinterest in her accomplishments as proof that her expectations for a marriage of mutual sharing were "weird and too idealistic." But like Sara McDevitt, Stephanie finally chose not to continue living in two worlds at once. In one world, she pleased Larry by hanging on to his every word, passively conforming to his idea of the good wife. Yet in another world, her own inner space, she questioned all that she appeared to accept. Slowly, Stephanie stopped the masquerade. After her divorce she began living a new, more integrated life.

For women in disintegrating marriages, gaining self-esteem is not always a matter of acquiring money, power, or education. A woman may possess all of these advantages and still lack self-worth because she trusts her husband's judgment more than she does her own. With difficulty a woman who has always respected her husband's wisdom will finally see that her capacity for self-assertion is compromised by his limitations.

Nancy Carlson, the debutante daughter of a wealthy southern family and Phi Beta Kappa graduate of a top-ranked university, ended her marriage by quietly accusing her establishment husband, "You have stolen my soul." The moral question raised for Nancy Carlson was how much longer she could remain married and still stay loyal to her own values. In the most personal way, her honor was at stake.

Throughout their marriage, Nancy and Martin Carlson had different interests. She preferred the symphony, ballet, and theater, while he gave his time to stocks, computers, and trout fishing. "But our differences in taste were never a problem to us," Nancy points out. "We just accepted that this was how we were, and sometimes went our separate ways."

Nancy might have been busy during the day, for example, organizing a fund-raising campaign for the museum, but at seven o'clock, cocktails and dinner were prepared at home, and, wearing a long skirt, she greeted her husband. Nancy's talents were respected in the community, but never in a way that stole the limelight from Martin.

But the balance became delicate when the governor of their southwestern state commissioned Nancy to redecorate the Capitol building with Native American art borrowed from regional museums. When the governor's staff called Martin to confirm his attendance at a private luncheon before the gala opening, Martin replied that he had better ways to spend his time. His demeaning attitude continued after Nancy was appointed state commissioner for the arts, administered a budget of ten million, and managed a staff of eighteen. Martin trivialized her efforts on behalf of the arts as insignificant and sometimes mocked, "You're not as smart as you think you are."

Nancy received accolades from throughout the Southwest but never enjoyed a private or public compliment from her husband. His disinterest at public functions embarrassed her, in fact. "He just pounded into me that what I was doing was not worthwhile," Nancy explains. "But it wasn't that he was verbally abusive. Much of it was through subtle body language and even silence. I had always respected his judgment; I wouldn't have married him otherwise. So my self-esteem just eroded."

Recognizing her depression, Nancy left with her teenage daughter for a university-sponsored tour of Rome, Florence, and Venice, where they enjoyed lectures by curators and scholars. Late one night, relishing her solitude and the stars over the Grand Canal, Nancy vividly recalls thinking, My God, I've got to get out of this marriage.

Typically, when she arrived home, Martin did not inquire about her trip. But Nancy, reinforced in the value of her work by her travels, responded to his wordless commentary with quiet determination: "You are destroying the core of who I am. You have stolen my soul. You have corroded my soul." Martin left their home that night.

The separation remained traumatic for Nancy, however. She continued as commissioner for the arts, but she also wanted a paying position. She was ambivalent about pursuing such prospects until reading Colette Dowling's *The Cinderella Complex*, which her twenty-year-old daughter gave her during a college visit. "The book had a strong message for me," Nancy reveals. "I knew immediately that I had to take life in my hands. I was not going to stand for a Prince Charming rescuing me!"

The very next day Nancy called a Santa Fe gallery specializing in auctioneering and appraising of art, antiques, and estates and said, "I understand that you are going to open an office in my city. If that's true, then I'm the one to do it." Nancy was hired. Her success was so astounding that within three years she became national executive vice-president of the appraising firm. Elated by her accomplishments, she comments, "My self-esteem is back; my soul is intact. The greatest gift I ever gave myself is myself."

Nancy's social register parents do not understand her need to work any more than they appreciate her Phi

Beta Kappa key or her master of fine arts degree. Yet if Nancy were to recycle her life, she would have had her own career from day one of her marriage: "Education in itself doesn't guarantee self-esteem. A woman has to have something which belongs only to herself, something that no one can take away from her. I wish I had known that at twenty." But if Nancy lacked such recognition, her daughter, who propelled her in new directions with *The Cinderella Complex*, does have the message.

Divorced women struggling to build new lives often benefit from their children's support in ways they never dreamed. One newly divorced woman, worried about maintaining ties with a teenaged stepdaughter whom she loves dearly, was reaffirmed by the girl's awkward gesture in asking her to be a chaperone for the junior prom. "It seems like such a simple thing," the mother relates with glistening eyes, "but it was her way of saying that things were all right between us."

In more complex ways, a child can become a role model for a divorced mother who is wrestling with new career demands. Trying to adapt to a reduced income and sort out her future, one woman was inspired by witnessing her daughter's adjustments. A college student, the young woman balanced a work-study job on campus with waitressing in a family restaurant in the evenings. With a full academic schedule that included an internship in city government, she maintained dean's list grades. "I was so proud of her ability to cope," her mother says, "that I was even more motivated to succeed myself. And she was never mean or resentful toward me because her life had changed so drastically. I could never let her down."

A fifteen-year-old boy squashed any doubts his mother had about walking out on his father: "A lot of people say they're going to do things but never do," he told her. "You're gutsy. You decided what you wanted to do and then did it without making a big deal. That's neat. You never belonged here anyway."

Women in the crisis of divorce value unexpected bon mots from their children, for in general they count upon other divorced women and professional therapists for emotional support. But it was not always this way. Only in the past twenty-five years, since the publication of *The Feminine Mystique*, have women been able to choose comfortably from a variety of options to support them through the cycle of divorce. Even women who disapproved of the women's liberation movement and dismissed consciousness-raising groups as nonsense have benefited. Women's liberation made it legitimate for them to discuss their marital problems, even if some women still refuse to credit its positive influence on their personal lives.

For example, one woman recovering from a shattered marriage was motivated in 1971 to organize the first divorce support group in her Episcopalian church because she felt confident that her loneliness was not unique. Sadly she recalls women at that time who dared not confide in other women because they saw their domestic problems as private failures: "A code of silence prevailed. Women I knew never exchanged secrets; never supported each other. I recognized my unhappiness in another young mother at the community swimming club. We would seek each other out, and watch our children play together, but we never said a word about our unhappy marriages because we thought they were totally our own fault. When we see each other now, we begin to cry about those days. Divorced women, even in the early seventies, were seen as pariahs."

In their efforts to be happy in marriages that appeared to be ideal, women projected images of being fulfilled wives and mothers, internalizing all responsibility for failures in their relationships. Virginia Gartley, age fifty-seven, always lived in a privileged home, working for pay only a few months as a secretary before her marriage in 1956. Yet as she struggled with suspicions about her husband's infidelity, she confided only in her housekeeper, "my best friend; she still is."

No one has priority in the business of helping divorced women through a cycle of affirmation. Neighbors, ministers, priests, religious counselors, lawyers, professors, psychiatrists, psychologists, and plain good friends can be sources of great comfort and encouragement to women who will admit that they need help. Women will also credit formal and informal support groups, women's studies courses, Al-Anon, and Alcoholics Anonymous for their renewal. A successful magazine editor still blesses the suburban neighbor who knocked at her kitchen door, camouflaging two glasses of cold martinis in a soup kettle, ready to hear about her first day of job interviews. Eight years after her divorce, a corporate vice-president has dinner monthly with three other women who divorced at the same time as she. "We're still a minisupport group for each other. Divorce is an experience you really never get over."

Divorced women who are happy with their personal lives and careers claim that their ability to be introspective and their willingness to communicate and be involved with others were essential factors to their achieving new meaning for themselves. Unlike the situation of even twenty-five years ago, a woman no longer has to deal secretly with her domestic problems but has the freedom to choose from a range of therapeutic experiences. For some, good friends are enough. Others, without feeling any stigma, want the support and structure of professional counseling.

Rita Menotti, age forty-three, has benefited from the culture's more enlightened attitude about the problems of divorced women. But barely a generation ago she might have been stumbling by the light of her own experience.

For an entire year Rita denied the fact of her husband's adultery because she simply did not know what she would do as a single parent with three children. Married twenty-two years to a prosperous optician, she had the "freedom to do whatever I wanted to do; I had no financial limitations, but I didn't have an education, either." When Rita learned about her husband's affair, she kept her knowledge a secret, even from him. She did seek counseling, however, and gave time to a community organization that offered tutoring services for handicapped children. On the advice of her counselor and the support of a coworker, she registered for a women's studies course at an urban women's college thirty miles from her home. The drive into the city was in itself a leap into freedom because "I never drove outside our small town, and certainly not on a freeway."

From the women's studies course and from her therapist, Rita drew courage to confront Bert, who then agreed to counseling and made promises for the future. As part of their new understanding, Rita would become a full-time college student, majoring in elementary education. But after two years Rita knew her husband's affair was rekindled. Bert tried to make amends by taking the family on a Caribbean cruise. Rita went, but she wasn't happy. "I couldn't regain trust. Oh, I suppose I could live out the rest of my life with him, but it would be a lie."

Completing requirements for her bachelor's degree, Rita has filed for divorce, "scared yet excited" about the future. "I could not have done this four years ago," she reflects, "but now I know I can earn money. I'll give up a lot—clothes, cars, vacations—but I'm happy with myself, and I know I can be strong for my kids."

One suspects that twenty-five years ago, Rita Menotti would not have sought psychological counseling; one knows that she would not have had a course in women's studies. Yet Rita is also aware that redirecting her life will be an ongoing struggle. Support systems in themselves cannot help women who will not actively participate in their own renewal.

Different from Rita is a woman who admits that she took advantage of every kind of therapeutic experience, including psychological counseling, therapy support groups, Children of Alcoholic Parents, and various workshops for divorced women sponsored by church, community, and university. But she never improved. Basically she was indulging in a morbid introspection, making her husband's betrayal of her the focal point of her life. Her search for self-confidence was futile until she recognized that the same message, dressed in a different vocabulary, was emerging from all of these sessions: "I finally absorbed that I am in control of me and how I behave. I make my own choices. I am not a victim and cannot blame anyone else for perpetuating the disappointment I feel about my life."

Once divorced women truly accept that they alone are responsible for the consequences of their actions, they free themselves to use their inner resources to begin again. Overnight results are never possible, however. "On the surface," Karen Sherman admits, "I looked as if I had it all together by the time I enrolled in law school. But when I had to talk with Jerry on the telephone about our daughter, I would wish he were dead, or at least would lose his job. When those thoughts stopped clouding my mind, I knew I had recovered."

Living through the crisis of divorce, a woman actually chooses whether or not she will grow in self-confidence. Divorced women who truly create and celebrate new lives have much in common. They welcome opportunities for attaining self-knowledge and self-awareness. They deal positively with anxiety, fight against despair, and risk challenges that will bring purpose and meaning to themselves and others. They initiate psychological and emotional support services and respond to the efforts of loyal friends and family. They act from a context of values that is based on trust in their own goodness. However strong the temptation, they guard against self-pity.

Women who triumph after divorce are not simpering Pollyannas, but hard-eyed realists who in the end confront truth and abandon self-delusion. They have faith in life but do not fool themselves with empty promises. The saving prince will not ride again. And Grace Kelly is dead.

CHAPTER 5

Marriage Redux

A second marriage is a volunteer program. And a good one is such a pleasure after a terrible first marriage.

Nancy Stewart
May 28, 1987

It is not only while in sync with the pristine rhythm of the rocking chair that a woman will discover that she is worth more than a rag doll. Sometimes this recognition also occurs when she is in the arms of a man other than her husband. Divorced women who are determined to build independent lives do not eliminate men from their design for the future. But when considering marriage, they vow to be more circumspect than they were the first time. Their attitude is expressed by Doris Minton, who earned a doctorate and became vice-president of a small university after her divorce: "I would not suffer one month in a marriage, let alone fifteen years. I like the company of men, and I would like to marry again, but not at all costs."

At the same time, women will admit their difficulty in shaking loose from the old fantasy that a handsome prince will, indeed, find the mate to their lost glass slipper. As much as they may want to rewrite the legend and drive their own chariot, the temptations are strong to play Cinderella once they begin the dating ritual. Starting law school after divorcing at age thirty-three, Margaret Peterson was committed to giving her career top priority. Yet, while dressing for her first "real date," she reverted to "all the things I had learned in *Seventeen*. I spent at least three hours making up my eyes. Then I realized what I was doing and thought, For God's sake, get a grip on." Divorced women who are determined to be responsible for their own futures will watch themselves sideways to guard against reactivating the self-image that their ultimate mission in life is to please the man who buys them dinner.

Now a partner in a small accounting firm, one woman admits that she kept her Cinderella fantasy alive for seven years after her divorce at age thirty-one. It would not die until she freed herself from seeing men as stereotypes rather than as "real people. I kept fitting the men I dated into slots. There was the old-monied Presbyterian, the nice Catholic, or the prosperous Jew. I wanted to fall in love. But I couldn't because I was always categorizing men through external factors, like their families, professions, businesses, houses, apartments, boats, you name it. I really wasn't seeing them as individuals. When I faced the fact that I wasn't going to be saved by a man, I felt a sense of real loss because I had always behaved on that premise. Once I examined the premise, I did fall in love and marry. It's just too bad that it took me seven years to figure out, finally with the help of a psychiatrist, what I was doing. It was only after I married that I went on for my MBA."

The effort of a divorced woman to break bondage with Cinderella can also be complicated by the hovering ghost of an ex-husband. Expecting a man to act as her former husband did, she will begin to react as she did with him. For example, a divorced woman, now secure in her own business, relates a humorous incident that occurred shortly after her separation. Invited by her dinner date to share his dessert, she stared at him without understanding and then registered disbelief. "A man who wanted to share! What a revelation it was to me. My husband would have said, 'I want it all.' " But the comic situation opened her eyes to the danger of the perception that all men are cut from the same mold. She feared that next she would be dating only men who cloned her husband; that way she could avoid risking vulnerability by knowing how to respond. Divorced women who recognize this tendency in themselves will sometimes seek professional counseling in an effort "never to make the same mistake again. Maybe I'll make other dumb mistakes, but not with a second marriage."

Maria Graham knows herself well after having completed therapy and the twelve rehabilitative steps of Alcoholics Anonymous. Although she would like to remarry, she does not actively seek out men. To avoid entering into another dependency relationship because of loneliness or fear, she cultivates the friendships of other women for the theater, symphony, shopping, or travel. "I'm not escaping men," she clarifies, "just not pursuing them." By following her own interests, Maria

101

feels that she will marry again. "If not, that's all right, too."

Margaret Peterson reveals that the first year after her divorce "it was a daily battle to live alone. Telephone conversations with other divorced friends returning home from work at six o'clock became very important to me. Those welcome-home calls made me feel that someone really cared how I had spent my day. Until I started law school, those voices on the telephone were my real family."

But some women treasure the sense of space that opens in their lives after divorce. They do not identify it with loneliness. Karen Sherman explains that "divorce has not turned me against men. Some days I think, Oh, yes, I want to marry again. Then at other times I just like my independence too much. I don't ever want to tailor my needs to accommodate someone else. Maybe a nice, long involvement is what I really want."

Playwright Sara McDevitt states matter-of-factly that she can't imagine remarrying or living with a man again because "I like my space." She explains, "This is the first time I have not had a central man of importance in my life. I broke off from a relationship four months ago. But even if I never have another one, I know I can feel like a complete human being. I like sex and I miss it a lot. But it's important for me to know that I can survive without it." She speculates, "Growing up, you had to have a man or you weren't complete. I was an RN at nineteen, but if I hadn't also been engaged, I would have been a failure."

Women who achieve in their own right after divorce no longer depend upon a man or marriage for personal validation. They are happy in the lives that they have chosen to live, as opposed to the marriages they entered into with misgivings or maintained because of loyalty, fear, blind trust, or insecurity. But that does not mean that they are cynical about men, marriage, or sex. For a woman who wants to forge her own identity, however, remarriage is never a priority. For example, after her divorce Nancy Stewart was simply happy to be alive and free to enjoy her children without fearing the intrusion of a drunken husband searching the house for her and yelling threats.

"The peace was heavenly," she describes. "A Friday night spent ice skating with the kids was better than any dinner at Lutece. I was never so happy. I just wanted to develop my business and give the kids a stable home life. I never thought about remarrying. I never gave any signals to men because I really didn't have any! In six years, I had only one brief relationship and not more than three dates." The man Nancy married was an old friend who was also divorced. They babysat for each other's children, and gradually their friendship and shared concern for the children grew into love. "In some ways," Nancy analyzes, "the relationship was free to develop because it was real safe. We were friends. I never looked upon marriage to provide salvation, and I still don't. A second marriage is a volunteer program. And a good one is such a pleasure after a terrible first marriage."

The experience of having had their first marriages

shatter does not mean that women necessarily grow jaded about the joys of married life. But those who have achieved faith in themselves at great price know that to seek salvation in a second marriage is simply to plunge right back into the mistakes of their past. "I really don't want to spend my life alone," says Rita Menotti. "But I certainly don't want to marry someone who will just make things easy for me. I had an easy life because I had everything material that I could want. I will never live a lie again just to have things." Only by securing her economic independence can a divorced women enable herself to keep such a pledge.

In a very painful way, Sandy Jeffries learned how her husband calculated her right to participate in family decisions: having no earned income, she had no voice. Graduating in 1966 from a New England university, Sandy married the president of the best fraternity on campus. "At the time," she remarks, "that was what one was supposed to do. I measured success by dollars and life-style, and Tom showed great potential. Now I know at age forty-four that all of that doesn't bring happiness. Careers were not encouraged for women then. Or if they were, I wasn't listening."

Tom developed a successful career as a consumer marketing specialist, traveling the world for long stretches of time while Sandy was home with their three children. When he lost his position, he didn't miss a beat finding another one that required the family to move to another state. Since other lucrative offers would have allowed them to stay in their New York home, Sandy asked why he didn't consider one of them.

His reply: "When you make the kind of money I make, then you can decide what we are doing." Hurt and demeaned, Sandy finally admitted that their marriage had been less than a partnership for a good many years. And from that point on, they never really talked about important matters.

In a new city, without grandparents or friends, the children had trouble adjusting to school and the neighborhood. Sandy began confiding in the divorced father of one of her daughter's classmates. Their friendship blossomed into a romance, and Sandy became even more aware of the caring and communication that was missing in her marriage. But when Tom learned of Sandy's affair, he filed for divorce, in accord with the language of the law, on the ironic basis of "alienation of affections."

At the time of the divorce, Sandy was frightened. Happy not to be married to Tom, she did not want to be "unmarried, either, because I didn't know how I would survive. My temptation was to find a rescuer, but I also knew if I took that route I would only hear again someday, 'When you make the kind of money I make, then you can decide what we are doing.'" Coming to terms with this possibility, Sandy became licensed to sell real estate, earning twenty-five thousand dollars her second year. "I have no great goals for myself like owning my own agency. I'm just relieved to know that I can support myself. I don't feel fear anymore. I don't need to get married. There's a big difference between needing to marry and wanting to marry. It's great to feel free enough to make that distinction."

Like Sandy Jeffries, Marian Kramer recognized the need to earn her own living before divorcing or marrying a second time. A dependent wife in her first marriage, Marian knew well the importance of having her own economic security. In fact, she delayed her divorce for many years because she did not know how she would otherwise support herself.

Marian blames her inability to withstand peer pressure as the reason for marrying Stan, "a medical student who was attractive and Jewish. All of my college friends were either engaged or married by graduation. I didn't like teaching, and in the midsixties I really didn't see any other options. But after six months, I knew our marriage would not work. Stan was always decent and kind; neither of us ever had an affair. Life was just terribly boring, but never painful enough to do anything about it. Our major satisfaction came from being together with our children, family, and friends. I spent ten years on the telephone commiserating long distance with a friend I seldom really ever saw."

At least eight years before her divorce, when her children were in school, Marian carefully began planning for her own financial stability. Her first step out of the house was to open a small card and candle store in an old building renovated by her father in a southern California beach community. Marian was the only one of her friends who was employed full-time, so she was constantly answering their concerns: "'But what about your tennis game? What about your volunteer work?' It was hard to fight their guilt trips."

Since the store never lost money in five years, Marian

developed confidence that she could eventually gain financial independence and leave Stan. Her goal was to make twenty-five thousand dollars annually to support herself because she figured that he would support the children. But the card and candle store could not earn a significant profit without a hefty financial investment, which she could not make. Marian's situation became more problematic when Stan's emotional depression, suffered intermittently over a span of years, worsened. "Since Stan was never a son of a bitch, I could not possibly leave him in such a defenseless condition."

Marian attended therapy sessions with Stan for the next few years in an effort to understand and cope with his illness. When the therapist finally encouraged her to see a psychiatrist on her own, Marian took three months to get up enough nerve to make an appointment. She reflects, "I realized that I had to figure out why I had been willing to stay married to Stan for so many unhappy years." Marian finally came to understand that her own self-image was enhanced by Stan's helplessness. By taking care of Stan and the children, and maintaining a business, she presented herself as a very strong person.

With this deeper understanding of herself, Marian was responsive to an unsolicited call from the executive director of a new drug rehabilitation program for teenagers in San Diego. New to the city, he did not know about Marian's domestic problems. But he had heard about her successes as a fund-raiser for community organizations and as a businesswoman. He urged her to apply for the position of development director. This offer from a stranger who did not know Stan occurred at the same time that Marian had made the break-through discovery that she was utilizing Stan's inade-quacies to make herself look better. She accepted the position when she was convinced that she had earned it on her own merits, not because she was known as the stoical wife of a needy man.

Confident that she had done all she could to help Stan, Marian filed for divorce after a year as develop-ment director. Her poor marriage, she claims, was as much her responsibility as the failure of it was Stan's.

Marian describes her second marriage, however, as being "too good to be true." For that reason she has rejected offers to leave the nonprofit sector for positions that would double her present salary of thirty-five thou-sand dollars. "I don't have ambitious professional goals. I treasure my life with Gene and want to have time just to be together without other pressures. I don't want to have to travel and spend nights and early mornings at meetings. I do enough of that now. There was never much joy in the house when Stan and I were married. I'm forty-six and healthy, and want to cultivate the really good partnership I have with Gene. But I some-times feel guilty that I'm selling out by not aggressively pursuing a more high-powered career."

For the past twenty-five years much has been written about the psychological development of women and their values. Traditionally women were expected to live for the other persons in their lives. Decisions were ready-made for them. But in challenging the rules and roles that had been prescribed for centuries as the behavior of a "good woman," women consciously began to determine their own futures with the freedom previously experienced only by men. More recent research by Harvard professor Carol Gilligan is presented in her book titled *In a Different Voice*. She points out that girls and women follow patterns of psychological moral development different from those of boys and men. But until very recently male development has always been treated as a human norm. Gilligan concludes that male development leads to valuing autonomy, separation, initiative, and independence. Female development leads to valuing relationships, nurturing, and bonding. Gilligan therefore raises the question: Does it mean that women are immature in 1988 if they strive to balance their commitment to others with their commitment to themselves? But the question is not merely academic when Marian Kramer expresses that she feels "guilty" for choosing not to give more time and energy to expanding her career at the expense of enjoying the pleasures of life with her new husband. Gilligan would have Marian affirm her values as strengths to be imitated, not as weaknesses to be hidden. It is an ongoing struggle for women to believe that they can choose to act differently from men and yet be equal to them.

Divorced women who succeed in their own careers vow never again to be financially dependent on a husband. But neither would they marry a man who did not offer emotional support and understanding of their work. One executive vice-president, on the brink of marriage, admits that she is careful and direct in asking questions of the man who will probably be her second husband. "I'm always interested in uncovering his attitudes and values because I've developed a great deal of self-worth, and I'm not about to sacrifice it." Once married, they plan to adjust their professional time to support each other's careers. They will be together, for example, when he gives papers at medical seminars. He will join her as she travels worldwide as an estate and art appraiser.

Perhaps men and women who have grown in self-knowledge from the travails of divorce approach a second marriage more willing to know, understand, and respect individual priorities. Knowing what love is not, they value what love is and appreciate what it truly means to share their lives. The really smart woman no longer disguises her intelligence to get a man; and the really secure man is not threatened by her success. Thus a divorced woman with a successful career will not see it as a female weakness if she admits that she enjoys a man's appreciation of her. For example, Christine Rush, a corporate executive, walked into her kitchen after work to find the electric coffeepot reduced to ashes because she had not unplugged it after breakfast. Still berating herself when her fiancé arrived for dinner, she was comforted when he held her face in his hands and said, "Repeat after me, 'I am wonderful. I am wonderful.'" The reality is that women do experience affirmation when men respond to their needs and also appreciate their accomplishments.

Consequently, a divorced woman can awaken to her personal dignity through a sexual affair if her ex-husband saw sex merely as an expression of his possession

of her. Or, as one assertive woman explained less eso-
terically: "My husband fucked; he didn't make love. So
I always felt inadequate, as if something were wrong
with me, until I had a wonderful relationship with a
man who really cared about sex being a sensual experience for me. In twenty years of marriage, I never
really ever knew what sex and love were all about."

On the other hand, another woman, an academic who
achieved professional recognition only after her divorce, claims that even in the worst days of their marriage, she and her husband had "great sex. Everything
else," she adds, laughing, "was terrible." Outside of
the bedroom, she felt demeaned because he thwarted
and belittled any of her intellectual achievements. He
demanded that her first priority be to "keep house."

Although sensual attraction can be impersonal and
satisfied by a partner one does not love, women admit
to feeling compromised in a marriage that has no other
communication. But sex can also be a catalyst for a
woman's developing sense of herself if she has lived in
a marriage where intercourse is an expression of her
husband's proprietorship.

A divorced woman who defines her own goals, cre-
ates her own status, and lives in peace approaches men
and marriage with open eyes. She questions, and even
defies, illusions and conventions that once seduced her.
She knows the effort she has invested in gaining confidence, courage, and self-esteem. No one knows better
than she that the wrong decision to remarry would only
renew her understanding of bitter disappointment.

CHAPTER 6

Street Smarts

> NORA. I haven't the least idea what'll become of me.
>
> HELMER. But you're my wife, now and wherever you go.
>
> NORA. Listen, Torvald—I've heard that when a wife deserts her husband's house just as I'm doing, then the law frees him from all responsibility. In any case, I'm freeing you from being responsible. Don't feel yourself bound, any more than I will. There has to be absolute freedom for us both. Here, take your ring back. Give me mine.
>
> Henrik Ibsen,
> *A Doll's House*, 1879

When Nora slammed the door of her husband's doll house, she had no money and little education, and she faced a legal code that valued wives as their husband's property. Times have changed, but women who exit their marriages as dramatically as Nora still have slim hope of making legal, financial, and educational systems work to their advantage. The best advice of divorce attorneys, financial consultants, psychologists, and divorced women concurs that women should plan ahead for divorce. Nora Helmer, on the other hand, hardly knew where she would sleep on her first night away from home: "I want to leave right away. Kristine should put me up for the night—" Ibsen's insight into a married woman's repressed freedom is brilliant, but wives who yearn to duplicate Nora's escape need to develop a street sense that prevents their ever having to say, "I haven't the least idea what'll become of me."

Women best prepare themselves for divorce by accepting responsibility for knowing the financial assets of their marriage from day one. The wife who asks no questions and receives a cash allowance from her husband each Monday morning is not yet an oddity. Even when generating their own incomes, women will trust decisions regarding finances solely to their husbands. Women who divorce, whether or not they initiate the proceedings, spend more money on fees when lawyers have to educate them regarding financial documents that must be found before their assets and liabilities can be inventoried. Generally, husbands have access to documents that wives do not even know exist. Lawyers' fees escalate when their time must be spent in depositions and interrogatories to discover financial facts that are necessary before a divorce case can go to trial. Consequently the more documents a wife can produce, the less expensive her divorce proceedings will be.

Ideally a wife should always know the economic profile of her marriage: income, investments, and debts. Furthermore she should know where to locate bank, brokerage and annual benefit statements, life insurance policies, and tax returns. The name of the couple's accountant should not be one of life's mysteries. A woman who has these facts is adult, not suspicious. Attorneys and financial advisers urge wives who do not have financial information at their fingertips to get it the first moment that they sense problems in their marriage, even if the divorce occurs years later or never happens at all.

Patricia G. Milligan, a certified financial planner and vice-president for Shearson Lehman Hutton, says plainly, "A wife should ferret out her husband's assets before the atmosphere gets hostile and things slip under the carpet. When in doubt, photocopy the 1040 tax return because that's the closest we can get to the truth of the total financial picture. From it, we can get clues as to where the money is. Even if you have a head full of steam and want to leave immediately, don't move until you are loaded with financial facts, have established your own credit, and are prepared emotionally to make responsible decisions." No matter who wants the divorce, once a wife has her first appointment with an attorney, she pays a high price for ignorance if court orders and motions are needed to smoke out her husband's financial assets.

A woman who is less than certain about the stability of her marriage should also realistically weigh her future economic security. The day she stops working outside of the home, her earning capacity erodes in comparison with her husband's. Courts are concerned that the division of assets be equitable, but a woman's vulnerability is in the long term disparagement between her income and her husband's. When a woman has left the work force, courts find it difficult to factor in her losses to bring about economic justice. A husband can generally make up his losses, whereas a wife usually has to live off her share of the financial distribution and reduce her life-style. No matter what her original earning potential, a wife rarely closes the gap with her husband after she gives up a career.

For example, a single woman without a college degree who earns thirty thousand dollars a year in middle management will not be able to return to a similar position after a lapse of years. Meanwhile her husband steadily advances in salary and accumulates retirement benefits. Women need to be savvy about long-range economic consequences when they are completely dependent upon their husband's earnings or accept splintered, part-time employment without accruing benefits.

Married women often lose out on retirement benefits by switching part-time jobs, particularly in public relations or sales positions. Concerned about flexible scheduling, they do not think about building nest eggs. If these women become ex-wives, they risk facing bleak retirement years because Social Security will not cover their expenses. "A divorced woman," says Peggy L. Ferber, Esq., a specialist in family law, "needs to learn to think about herself first. Sometimes after a divorce settlement, this can mean delayed gratification for her, meaning that she should buy an annuity so that a pension, if she has one, and Social Security are not her only forms of income. Also she wants to think about her adult children. It may be better for her to have disability rather than life insurance, so that she doesn't become a burden on them." Women who divorce need to think realistically about many aspects of their retirement years.

Patricia Miller, Esq., a divorced mother who began law school at age thirty-nine and now specializes in family law, exhorts: "It is devastating to become an economically dependent adult. Without thinking too much about it, young women quit work after marrying and having children. Yet they can't return after twenty years to where they were, and the legal system can't make them whole again. They can't become surgeons or get back on the corporate executive track. The woman who does is most unusual. The reality is that even her Social Security is fifty percent of her husband's, and that's provided only if she has been married to him for ten years. She has no accrued retirement benefits. If she followed her husband to a new city, maybe she did work part-time, but her career has no continuity. Even if she is lucky enough to have pension benefits from part-time employment, they are little compared with her husband's. Besides that, she was probably carried on her husband's health insurance policy. Even though corporations now have to carry divorced spouses for three years at the same rate it costs them, the fact remains that the spouse has to pay during that time. Yet women give up or compromise very desirable careers with very little thought about these realities."

But a woman should think differently about her economic future after divorce, even when maintaining a career. If used to a double income, a married woman frequently is not ambitious about advancing professionally because location, stability, and convenience may be her priorities. Even after divorcing, a woman can lock herself into a dead-end job out of a sense of loyalty to employers. But will they really be hurt if she leaves? Can she afford to stay in the same job without depriving herself and her children? A divorced woman often needs to reeducate herself in the male style if she is going to fulfill her economic potential.

In households where the husband is the only or chief breadwinner, a wife can best prepare for divorce by planning to increase her earning power. For example, a woman who wants to start a catering business should begin culinary school before announcing a decision to divorce. Likewise, if two years short of earning a bachelor's degree, she should enroll immediately in college courses. If a woman defines her goals and is enrolled in an educational program before filing for divorce, then the courts will continue her tuition and often maintain baby-sitting expenses until she completes the requirements.

If she plans ahead, a woman at the start of divorce proceedings can present a clear plan to an attorney regarding her goals and the financial support she will need to fulfill them. Women who have no scheme for their futures are generally advised by attorneys to begin to prepare themselves for careers before they divorce. Courts are not sympathetic to arguments, for example, that a mother with young children must stay at home. A full-time job may not be necessary, but she must show some effort toward developing self-reliance. If a

woman is embarked on a defined program, from neurosurgery to cosmetology, "and light exists at the end
of the tunnel, then any divorce attorney worth his salt
should get her what she wants," concludes a seasoned
lawyer in family practice.

Further schooling is also ideal for a young mother
because flexible scheduling is generally possible and
child care facilities are common on campuses. Many
kinds of financial assistance are available to older
women, so-called nontraditional students, who want to
continue their interrupted undergraduate study or begin
college courses for the first time. In fact, mature women
are welcome on campuses because the eighteen-year-
old population is continuing to decline. A visit to any
college campus will reveal that many older students are
enrolled in classes. A woman should investigate ad-
missions policies, financial aid plans, and academic programs at colleges and universities in her area. Usually
a special office exists on campus where competent
professionals counsel and support women who want to
return to school.

But the most credible advice often comes from a
woman in similar circumstances, one who has begun or
returned to college classes. Cindy Ferres, mother of two
young sons, is a year from graduating with a degree in
history and secondary education from a women's college. Married at age twenty-nine, she willingly gave up
an annual salary of thirty thousand dollars as a manager
of flight attendants for a major airline. After ten years
of conflict and tension, Cindy wanted to divorce but
knew that she could not return to a similar managerial

position without a bachelor's degree. So she moved back to her hometown where her family lived and enrolled in a local college. Her husband fumed that her decision was based solely on her gaining more child support, but the court did not agree with him.

After graduation, Cindy is practically assured a position as a high school history teacher. But returning to school offered her other benefits besides career preparation. "I began to focus on my future and let go of the past. My divorce was no longer the center of my life. For the first semester, I had a need for confidantes. And a college campus with nontraditional students offers instant camaraderie. But it's interesting to watch divorced women students outgrow that need after a while. Divorce becomes a boring topic of conversation when you've just come out of an exciting class. Women begin to look ahead and don't want to think about how bad they once had it. Actually, the academic calendar almost forces you to think and plan ahead. It becomes more important to aim for the future than to keep the past alive."

Nontraditional students are also welcome in college classrooms because they do well academically. Their work and life experience can even be converted into academic credit if they take the standardized College-Level Examination Program (CLEP), which is administered on the third week of each month at more than 1,500 educational institutions throughout the United States. A student who tests well in general course areas can receive credit toward her degree. Again, such information is readily available through campus counselors who advise nontraditional students.

Because it can be a buyer's market in higher education, divorced women should be aggressive about seeking information and comparison shopping. A financial aid officer will inform any potential student about educational grants and loans available from the federal government, as well as tuition discounts and special packages unique to the college. But a woman in divorce proceedings should also check out options in her community. Organizations often provide financial assistance for students who satisfy very specialized criteria regarding ethnic origin or religious affiliations. Women's business and professional groups frequently support women who want to return to school. The librarian at a community or university library should be helpful in recommending numerous directories and guides, such as *A Woman's Guide to Career Preparation: Internships, Grants and Loans* by Ann J. Jawin.

To unearth all of this information requires time, effort, and a willingness to ask questions. Again, a woman who knows that divorce is inevitable and wants to continue her education increases her advantages by planning ahead.

Women who want out of marriages are usually pragmatic about setting goals and seeking career counseling. Wives who are surprised by husbands who want divorces generally have to work harder at building their self-confidence. Nonetheless, divorce attorneys will deliver the same message to both types of women: Identify your skills and interests; define what you want to do;

figure out the best way to go about it, and get going.

Attorneys give a great deal of advice to their divorce clients. A woman therefore wants to make sure that she chooses a lawyer whose judgment she trusts and "whose style you like," adds Gail Kilborn, who left her first attorney because he was "too dear and gracious. When he understood that I was really serious about divorcing my husband, whom he knew, he said, 'Gail, if Clinton realized you were here today, he would be very hurt.' And he had the nerve to say this after having heard my full story! After eighteen years, Clinton suggested that we have a marriage of convenience. For three months I sat on a chair, immobilized. Then when I finally faced that I had to see an attorney, I was devastated that he was more concerned about my husband's feelings than my welfare. I decided that I didn't need someone so sensitive to represent me."

Attorneys who patronize women foster their dependency. For her divorce, a woman has a right to expect competent representation from an attorney who will give her all the information necessary for her to make informed decisions. If she can afford the cost, she should consider interviewing attorneys to ascertain how they will involve her in the process. To begin, she wants to determine if the lawyer is committed to the divorce process as an opportunity for her to develop independence and self-reliance. Will she be included in final meetings with her attorney, accountant, and actuary regarding financial distribution? If the lawyer looks askance at being presented with questions, perhaps she should seek another one to represent her. Only the client herself will ultimately pay for the cultivation of her helplessness.

During an initial interview with an attorney, a woman must be clear about her expectations regarding other issues as well. Will the lawyer who interviewed her work on the case? Will she have access to the attorney or communicate through a paralegal? What is the fee structure? Sitting on the lawyer's side of the desk, Patricia Miller claims, "If a woman comes to me and says, 'Wake me when this is over—just tell me where to sign,' then I say, 'Get another lawyer. If I catered to that attitude, I would be doing you a disservice.'"

Although the best attorneys representing women in divorce cases want to develop their client's self-confidence, attorneys are not therapists. "I always tell my clients," says Peggy L. Ferber, "that I am sympathetic and compassionate. But I am their lawyer, and not their best friend or counselor." Divorce attorneys will recommend psychological counseling, but their own primary interest is in attaining a just economic settlement for their clients.

For example, when Gail Kilborn's husband told her that he wanted a marriage of convenience, she remembers thinking, "I need a therapist, and I also need a lawyer. Somehow I knew that I had to seperate the two. If you expect a lawyer to hold your hand, then fees will escalate because the hours are longer. Besides that, a lawyer isn't really equipped to offer psychological support, and you are likely to become a nuisance."

But sometimes the advice of a therapist and an attorney can be contradictory. One woman remembers her therapist urging that she sue for support, whereas her attorney was confident that the best possible settlement had been negotiated and that a court battle would jeopardize it. But another woman claims her therapist accused her attorney of being too adversarial. "That's right," interprets a lawyer specializing in divorce. "A therapist's role is to concentrate on the emotional state of the patient. The lawyer's role is to protect the client economically. Lawyers are adversarial because divorce is an adversarial situation: the more the wife gets, the less the husband gets. His interest is adverse; there's no other way to describe it. I try to give my client a complete understanding of the facts, as a third party—the judge—will see them. If she is not going to do worse with a settlement, then she can't be afraid of going to court. If she does go to court, then she is taking a position which is adversarial to her husband's. Therapists are not lawyers, and lawyers are not therapists."

Although most women do not have trouble making this distinction, others do and are perplexed by it. Women going through divorce who are simultaneously in therapy or counseling should be aware that it is possible for them to experience this tension. Nonetheless, divorce attorneys strongly recommend that women should have psychological support while in divorce proceedings.

From the beginning, therefore, it is important for a woman to choose an attorney she trusts and respects. Gail Kilborn left her first attorney because his sensitivity quotient was too high toward her affluent husband, when she had not a penny to her name after twenty years of marriage. She could not even reclaim her inheritance because of having signed it over to her husband. However, she questioned friends and carefully pruned the grapevine to choose her second attorney. Gail was immediately impressed with his competence, but she had sudden insight that he was her ally on the morning of the afternoon her case was going to court.

After a three-hour conference, Gail, her attorney, and her accountant split for lunch before meeting at the courthouse. She noticed the attorney, with a handful of pink telephone messages to read, slip into a spartan deli. "It's funny, but at that moment I knew I was in the right hands. I figured that Clinton and his lawyer had also been meeting all morning. The difference was that if I had stayed with my first lawyer, he and Clinton's lawyer would have been settling the case over a gourmet lunch at a downtown club. It was a fleeting image, but I knew I had a real advocate."

A friend gave Gail $2,500 so that she could retain the lawyer she wanted. Women who are left penniless or with little revenue should "borrow and beg to retain the best attorney they can," is common advice from divorced women. Asked how she remained patient for seven years waiting for her divorce settlement, a woman who now manages her own small kitchenware business counsels: "After my husband left our home, I really didn't need anything. He kept paying all the bills. He was so willing to offer to divide the property and give me the house and car that we figured he was holding out on investments that I didn't know existed. The less anxious I appeared about it, the more I finally had to negotiate. With a court order, a settlement was forced, and I ended up very well."

Wives will often settle too quickly for the "house and car" when their husband's assets are substantial. On the other hand, wives can also pressure their lawyers to pursue settlements that are unfair. A good lawyer will uncover the husband's total worth and inform the client of the facts so that she plays with a full deck when making a decision regarding the lawyer's best and final advice about her settlement. Lawyers will not encourage a woman's blind trust if they value divorce as an educative process for her. Neither will they advise a client to steer a collision course if they think that her demands are unrealistic. But it is always a client's option to accept or reject her attorney's advice. If she chooses the latter, she usually has to begin again with a new attorney of her choice.

Women who cannot afford an attorney can be referred to one by calling the local chapter of the American Bar Association, where qualified lawyers donate their services. Some women determine that they do not want legal representation for their divorces and decide to proceed *pro se*, meaning they represent themselves. It is possible for couples who have little shared property, or who have distributed it by mutual consent, to process their own divorce papers without the benefit and expense of attorneys. This is a decision of grave consequences, however. Divorce proceedings are complex relating to child custody, support, and equitable distribution of property. By self-representation, a woman can lose on important issues that will affect her forever.

Over thirty grass-roots organizations across the country, under the umbrella of the National Child Support Advocacy Coalition, offer detailed information for persons who want to file for their own divorces. They also offer information and assistance on issues of child support and custody for persons unable to afford an attorney. Generally these groups have little funding and are maintained by urban saints who volunteer their time, often helping illiterate women to understand the court system and referring them to community organizations responsible for employment and housing problems and psychological and financial counseling.

For example, in Allegheny County, Pennsylvania, the organization SUPPORT was founded in December 1979 by Rose Palmer-Phelps, a mother with two young children who after her divorce had problems with child support. Originally operating out of her home with money raised from bake sales, SUPPORT has grown into an agency that in 1987 offered information and assistance to 4,500 persons on problems relating to separation and divorce, child support, and parenting. One of SUPPORT's clients was a ninety-year-old wife, understandably distraught that her eighty-five-year-old husband had left her for a nineteen-year-old woman.

SUPPORT is a superb example of grass-roots child support advocacy organizations throughout the United States. But in 1988 Rose Palmer-Phelps was one of only twenty-five women nationally to receive a Clairol, Inc., Take Charge Award as a model of courage. She refers to divorce as "America's number-one social disease that attacks any age or income level." Her best advice to women is to break out of a dependency pattern. "I try to convince women that it is better for them to survive alone than to go back to Mother. I try not to lose patience when young women say that they cannot work and also go to school. Women have to take charge of their lives, no matter what their income level."

Whatever her economic life-style, for example, a woman facing divorce should establish credit in her own name. She must start somewhere to build a credit history, even if she opens a bank account with birthday money or transfers it from the food budget. If necessary, she should consider borrowing from the bank and use the money itself to pay the loan back. Her first plastic may not be from American Express, but she can begin to establish her own credit with a local department store, a gasoline company, or a national chain of medium-priced retail stores. When problems occur in a marital relationship, investments and bills can be neglected. Once a woman has her own credit, she has some borrowing power and can separate herself from her husband's debts. If she does not want her husband to know that she has credit, she can have her mail delivered to a post office box.

A vice-president and credit manager of a major midwestern department store points out that credit is readily available for all persons, including divorced women. But when delinquent department store accounts are listed under both names, husband and wife are responsible until the debt is resolved. A divorced woman seeking credit will then have to endure a more complex procedure if she and her ex-husband are still fighting about settling bills. Computer systems will immediately identify the ex-wife as a poor credit risk. But credit managers advise that a customer should invest time in drawing attention to her special situation because computer scoring systems do not accommodate exceptions. Women too readily accept their poor credit ratings without appealing beyond the clerk who scores their applications. A direct inquiry to the credit manager is not out of the question. A divorced woman with a poor credit rating should also exercise her special circumstances, which is then included in the dossiers in all the credit bureaus in her community.

Nonprofit community agencies that are members of the National Foundation for Consumer Credit, Inc., exist across the United States to offer free and confidential credit counseling to consumers with incomes ranging from poverty level to six figures. Workshops on consumer credit are consistently sponsored by community colleges, for example. No matter what their level of income, women facing divorce need to be aware of establishing credit and managing money. Without risking utter dependency and poverty, women cannot abdicate responsibility or delay action regarding their financial situation.

Even though Heather Stowe worked as a financial analyst for a major brokerage firm during her marriage, she admits having felt "scary" about her own investments at the time of her divorce. "My husband had the larger of our two incomes. I knew my assets and liabilities, but I still had to draw a deep breath when I realized I was going to be on my own, for my income had diminished by two-thirds. I wasn't salaried, so I had an incentive to work harder. But it still was traumatic for me to take such responsibility. I really identify with the angst of decision making experienced by divorced women who are managing money for the first time, and possibly have more money than they ever imagined under their control."

Early in the process of divorce, a woman should educate herself to face decisions about how she will manage her financial settlement. If her understanding is at square one regarding joint property, the stock market, and certificates of deposit, she can begin to learn the vocabulary of financial planning by reading *Money* magazine and the business section of the local paper before graduating to *The Wall Street Journal*. Magazines like *Lear's* and *Savvy* direct articles to women who want to understand their investment options. A woman who could not afford the luxury of buying magazines and extra newspapers recommends choosing the longest line at the supermarket checkout to scour the racks and read such articles while waiting.

"A woman doesn't have to devote her life to taking care of her money," offers Barbara H. Behrend, vice-president and certified financial planner for Shearson Lehman Hutton, "but she does have to know enough not to be intimidated by brokers who really don't want to take the time to make sure she understands why certain advice is given. A woman on her own has to question, 'Why is this good to do? Why isn't this good to do?' And after she chooses how her money will be invested, she must monitor it; it's a consistent monitoring process."

If a divorced woman has a property settlement over $25,000, she should consider engaging the services of a professional financial planner, preferably one who will not allow her to be too trusting. Their first conversation will help her to decide her cost of living. Generally a client should expect a proposal to select her investments by the third meeting. "Sometimes women have to recognize that they can no longer buy Armani suits; other times they find it hard to believe that they don't always have to buy the cheapest wine," offers a financial planner who advises many divorced women. She tells about one who earned $15,000 a year but had no idea that her husband made well over $300,000. Accustomed to budgeting a telescoped weekly allowance, she could not even imagine a higher standard of living based on receiving five-digit monthly checks.

Not every divorced woman may need or want to have the services of a certified financial planner, but only a foolish woman would not arrange her finances to provide for her ultimate security, including retirement. If she is employed, the company credit union and human resource department can be sources for investment information, as well as the accountant who prepares her tax returns. But the sad fact remains that the less money a woman has, the less time a financial adviser will spend with her.

In the final analysis, a divorced woman cannot expect anyone else, not even paid professionals, to care about her problems as much as she does herself. The best that she can do is to discover and draw upon the most competent legal and financial resources available to her ability to pay.

When entering into second marriages, women in general find it awkward, during this most romantic period in their new relationship, to negotiate a prenuptial agreement. But when they earn high incomes because of their own hard work, they do put sentimentality aside to insist upon them. "Women have to learn to think with their heads, not their hearts," urges Barbara Reed, the owner of a multimillion-dollar real estate company in Maine. "I've worked too hard to build up what I have, and I don't want to see it slip through my fingers." Nancy Stewart, the manager of her own insurance company and the mother of three college students, arranged a prenuptial agreement that protects her assets for her children at the time of her death. But Elizabeth Hampsey, a successful attorney, who married a millionaire after having been divorced for ten years, is more extreme with a prenuptial agreement that asks nothing from her husband, even in the case of divorce.

Virginia Gartley knows she is from a generation before women's liberation but would never think to remarry without a prenuptial agreement. Divorced five years ago from a husband who had a string of affairs, Virginia is the ultrafeminine woman with a vein of iron. She has no intention of ever working. Born to southern gentry, Virginia, against her father's best judgment, married an enterprising young eastern businessman. Soon ensconced in a twenty-room house on Philadelphia's Main Line, she enjoyed a private plane, a small yacht, and five cars. "After being a hostess for over twenty-five years, I deserved everything I could get from my marriage."

Virginia won a divorce settlement of one million dollars, plus the house. She hired an accountant and invested in stocks. Now she would like to marry again because "since Noah's ark it's been two by two." Virginia likes the fact that her financial independence gives her the autonomy to date "men of caliber freely because they know I don't want their money. I'm also free from granting sexual favors because I don't need anyone to take me out to dinner." A prenuptial agreement is an important condition of Virginia's decision to remarry because she wants to ensure that her children will be the heirs to her estate. Likewise, she would expect a future husband to protect his own children with one.

A cynical attitude is no preparation, but a woman begins to face the complexities of divorce when she enters into marriage, whether for the first or second time, as a self-reliant, self-supporting, defined individual unwilling to abdicate those qualities. But in their absence, when the time arises, she must develop the street sense necessary to negotiate her own self-interests if she is to survive the worst days and secure her future.

CHAPTER 7

Heartfelt Advice

Keep your shit off the streets.

Anonymous

Divorced women who launch new lives feel an obligation to offer positive advice to women who are where they once were. They agree that marriages are worth saving and that wives and husbands should try to work out their differences. When this is impossible, a woman must think first about herself.

Although their messages cannot be reduced to simple prescription, divorced women agree that wives should be as economically independent and as financially savvy in a marriage as they possibly can. As a start, women should want to be trained or educated to support themselves. Says one woman who stopped working after her first child was born and stayed with her husband for fifteen years mainly because she did not know how she would support herself and her children: "Women who are not able to make their own living are like children. Even if it isn't a fancy living, it gives a woman the freedom to say, 'Hey, I don't like it here, and I don't have to put up with any abuse.'"

When divorced women admit the mistakes of their

135

own lives so that other women will not repeat them, they consistently say that women must aim to be self-sufficient. Lamenting the college courses not completed; the graduate degree not begun or the professional career cut short; recalling the years spent chauffeuring children to ball games and ballet lessons, entertaining their husband's business friends or protecting his ego from the imprint of their intelligence; remembering years of part-time jobs that contribute to erratic resumes and the energy invested in moving and decorating new homes—divorced women mourn lost opportunities to furnish their own souls and expand their own worlds. From firsthand experience they know how wives feel who lack self-confidence in their ability to earn money. They understand wives who distract themselves from confronting serious marital problems because they lack the economic freedom to decide their own destiny. Consequently divorced women who take pride in their accomplishments say without qualification, "Women have to prepare themselves to live in this world responsibly and independently. Only self-sufficient women have freedom and options."

Divorced women defend the right of any woman to be a career wife, but they are adamant that child rearing and housekeeping should not excuse her from being able to support herself. For example, Karen Sherman was scared when she picked up her two-year-old daughter and left her husband: "I needed to feel strong, but I had no education and did not want to live on a minimum wage." But with the help of student loans that she pursued, Karen was able to begin college courses and eventually finish law school. "Overwhelmed" when she thought about the long road ahead of her, Karen coped with anxiety by measuring her life into semesters: "I didn't look at the whole picture, just one semester at a time." Karen advises women: "It's better to go to school at forty or fifty than to wish at seventy that you had."

But women who are college graduates can be just as insecure about their futures as Karen Sherman was. A liberal arts graduate of a Seven Sisters college and the faculty wife of a tenured professor at an eastern university, Millie Heid knew that she had to become self-sufficient when her marriage was in trouble. Just as she was looking forward to spending a sabbatical year in Italy with her husband and three young children, Henry told her that he wanted a divorce. She thought he was experiencing a midlife crisis, but when their year abroad provided no romantic cures, Millie and Henry coolly faced her future. They decided that the best way to make divorce affordable for Millie was for her to benefit from free tuition and enroll in the university's degree program for a master of arts in teaching. After completing the requirements in a year and a summer, Millie was hired as a high school history teacher and moved with her children, all under the age of ten, from their rambling faculty house into a small apartment. Couples are seldom so pragmatic in designing together a future for a divorced wife. A rational decision did not soothe Millie's pain and the time she needed to heal, however. But nine years later she is director of development for a New England preparatory school. She is also happily remarried.

Women like Millie who developed successful careers after divorce consistently urge young women to find a larger identity outside the roles of wife and mother. Divorced women of the 1980s deliver different messages about marriage to their daughters, for example, than the ones they heard from their own parents of the forties, fifties, and sixties. They assume that their daughters will finish college and take pride in their careers. Their own parents generally valued higher education as important for ensuring that young ladies would fulfill themselves as affectionate wives and noble mothers married to prosperous men, becoming, like Princess Grace, the ultimate volunteer. "I don't want Megan simply to grow up, marry, and have babies," says Virginia Gartley, who now lives on a hearty divorce settlement after having given thirty years of her life to being the perfect corporate wife. "I never thought divorce would happen to me. I would have preferred to walk into the sunset years with the father of my children. Despite the fun I'm having and the freedom I now feel, I would have preferred my marriage to have worked. But when it doesn't, then get out." Virginia never worked during her marriage, but now she advises: "Marriages are more successful when each person has an identity, a career. I never imagined that I would ever think that way. I took it for granted that I would go from my father's care to my husband's."

If a wife is completely dependent upon her husband for financial support, she should at least have total knowledge of their economic situation, understanding how every penny is earned and where it goes. Few men are kind when getting a divorce, but women contribute to the decline of their own standard of living by drawing a blank on the financial picture of their marriages. In the words of Barbara Reed, "Women have to know about their husband's insurance policies, medical insurance, retirement benefits, and investments. If they act like bubbleheads during the marriage, they will be treated like bubbleheads through the divorce proceedings and at the crucial time of financial distribution." Divorced women know well that it is they who experience an abrupt change in life-style when their marriages end. They confide that they want other women to benefit from the mistakes of their ignorance and passivity. They counsel that women must be conversant about the details of the financial assets of their marriages if they want to do more than throw themselves on the mercy of attorneys and accountants who are negotiating their futures.

Barbara Reed continues, "And they (women) have to pay for good advice. Get the best lawyer and make it your business to understand what he or she is advising. If you truly don't like the advice, then get another good lawyer. But don't be dumb. Stupidity won't get you a dime."

Stupidity and shortsightedness do not earn friends, either. Newly divorced women often feel that they are entirely on their own to cope with survival. Yet women who start businesses or continue interrupted careers are frequently able to do so because they finally grow confident about approaching the "right people." Good friends of one divorced woman made her a big sign that read, "ASK! ASK for help! ASK for the job! ASK for the order!" Marital status has never handicapped a man from conferring on Wednesday with a banker he met on Saturday while playing golf. Yet a divorced woman who successfully managed someone else's dress shop when she should have owned her own admits that she "couldn't tell anyone about getting a divorce until Ann Landers got one, too." Divorced women who now know better counsel their peers to cultivate friends and friends of friends when they are trying to start new careers. They strongly urge that women imitate male behavior in focusing their vision, identifying and involving those persons who are in positions to help them achieve their goals.

But a divorced woman cannot move forward in this direction if she is consumed with exposing the "bad hand I was dealt." To seek help from others is not to weep at the feet of anyone who will listen and wail, "What shall I do with my life?" Phyllis Corbett, who attempted suicide because she felt alone and helpless while going through divorce proceedings, is tough with her answer. Now earning $150,000 a year as a corporate vice-president, she admonishes: "Wallowing in self-pity, anger, and despair is easy, often comfortable. It is also a waste of precious time and reinforces pain. The objective is to do the best you can to win with the cards you're holding, and then, win or lose, move on!

You certainly have no chance of winning the hand if you don't play it. Only an immature child throws in the hand, shouting, as I almost did, 'I quit.'"

To get to the stage where they can "play the hand," women do need to diffuse their anger and nurture their pain. Many divorced women recommend professional counseling when one is at the stage of sobbing, "What should I do with my life?" or, "How did this happen to me?" At the same time they urge women to change therapists if they feel they are not a match. In general women are vulnerable and filled with self-doubt when seeking counseling about domestic troubles. If they do not respond to their therapist, they are therefore quick to blame themselves. For example, a young married woman who was terribly unhappy in her third year of marriage was asked by the psychologist at their first appointment: "Why are you here?" When she could not really respond, he helped her by asking, "Do you want a divorce?" She simply answered, "No," and never returned. "It was a mistake that I did not turn to another therapist, but I didn't realize that I could shop around." Although she stayed with her husband for seven more years, she regrets not having left him when she first recognized their problems. But when she did finally separate from him, she had an emergency appointment the very next day with a psychiatrist, with whom she continued for a year. "It was the best money I ever spent. The process was painful but exciting. My confidence level was so low that I had to discover positive things about myself. But most of all I came to recognize that I am drawn to needy men, and I have learned not to be so accommodating." This woman concludes that counseling was absolutely imperative to rebuilding her self-esteem and preventing her from being one of those "bitches who make it a career to hate men."

A range of therapeutic options is available for the divorced woman who wants to grow in self-confidence. She should feel neither strong nor inferior because she chooses professional therapy. Divorced women insist that their peers should be comfortable to choose support systems that work best for them. Some women can rally by depending upon a sympathetic, nonjudgmental friend. One woman claims that her most perceptive listener was a gay man who gave her the best advice: "You are going through a terrible time, but keep your shit off the streets. If you need help, you know where to find it." Women who confide their domestic problems to three hundred of their most intimate friends usually end up embarrassed or, at best, confused by conflicting opinions or insensitive remarks. "When you see that your friends get a look in their eye when you arrive on the scene, then perhaps it's time to seek more structured support, like private counseling or organized therapy groups," recommends a divorced woman who is a psychologist. A corporate executive officer offers more jaded advice: "You cannot tell a person your problems more than once and expect to remain friends." Kissing her daughters good-bye in the morning, she sent them off to school with the admonition, "Heads up and shoulders back. We'll do our crying together at home tonight." But this same woman also knows that there is no "quick fix for loneliness." And the signal that one is recovering from the pain of divorce occurs when the "highs are not as high and the lows are not as low."

Women who choose to divorce might think that it will not hurt, but divorce "always brings an incredible series of losses in its wake," offers Stephanie Vogel, who speaks from her own experience and as a counselor to divorced women. To be able to begin a new career or discover new skills is certainly not the total answer to recover from divorce. For example, with her husband's help, Millie Heid became self-supporting as a high school history teacher, but economic security did not heal her emotional scars. She says simply, "I was hurt, and it was a long time before I could even think of dating again." For three years she focused her energy solely on her children and her job.

Stephanie Vogel continues: "I would urge women who are in the process of divorce to anticipate that they will experience grief, just as if there were a death. That pain needs to be expressed and shared with someone. Divorced women cannot greet a new life until they say good-bye to an old life." She cautions that divorced women will sometimes try to assuage their grief by immediately becoming involved with another man. But until they have completely mourned the past, divorced women will only postpone getting on with a new life if they court romances that are premature.

Practical advice is also offered by Carole Devlin, divorced for four years and the mother of six young adults, who became a successful market analyst after devoting most of her married life to promoting her husband's political career. She labels the time after divorce as a "transition period that no one can possibly like because, no matter what, it marks the end of certainty. And one has to grieve for the loss of certainty. It takes time to start a new life; it doesn't happen overnight." After divorce, she maintains, "a woman has to expect to feel bad and sad, and she needs to be comforted. The day after divorce is not how she will feel for the rest of her life. And when she gets through this transition, she will be stronger."

So that her advice does not sound like a series of pious platitudes, Carole continues to explain: "After divorce, it helps if you can identify precisely why you feel lonely or sad. If it is because you are poor, then think about others who are more poor and give some time to helping them. Volunteer time in a soup kitchen, for example. If you are lonely because you don't have your family, then think about those who are more lonely. Volunteer to feed patients in a nursing home. If you think that life is not fair, then visit children in a hospital or read to the blind."

Carole Devlin refers to the "caretaker muscles" that divorced women can learn to use in new ways. For example, holidays can be especially hard for parents who have joint custody of children. If a woman grieves for the Thanksgiving dinners that once were, she can celebrate the day with mothers and children living in a shelter. Carole's own most difficult time of day is between six and seven o'clock, when her family had dinner together. Now she programs her volunteer work into that time. Watching young mothers, she knows how low they can feel on Saturdays when their children visit with their fathers. Carole urges mothers who dread despondent Saturdays to think of that day as a gift and plan definite activities for it. "If mothers wait until children say good-bye before deciding what to do with the afternoon, they will do nothing because they feel so glum. They have to learn to substitute for those feelings of lost family life, and what might have been if..."

In summary, Carole feels that a woman can help herself recover from the emotional losses of divorce by knowing her needs, nurturing herself, and expressing herself in ways that bring meaning to the lives of others. Once the scenes of her marriage stop replaying in her mind's eye, she will be able to help other divorced women who are farther behind in their recovery than she. And in doing so, she will appreciate just how far she herself has come.

This period of transition after divorce can be productive for women who are willing to be reflective. During this time, some women rediscover the freedom of simple pleasures. Mothers relish the peace they enjoy living alone with their children, for example. "I always accepted as truth that children need a father," reveals a woman who tried for years to hide her husband's alcoholism from the public and her family. "But that's hogwash. What children need is stability and sanity. When my husband and I separated, I just loved the peace that descended on the house. Women shouldn't hang on to bad marriages for the sake of the children. It only gets worse."

A medical social worker who managed all of the household expenses was still insecure about leaving her husband, even though her annual earnings outstripped his and he spent little time with the children. The first months after their separation, she gained confidence simply by taking a vacation with her young family and pitching a tent by herself. "Doing something as commonplace as that contributed to my having a better sense of who I am, and what I can accomplish."

Other women displace their sadness and increase self-knowledge by reading about divorce and attending support workshops, including informal classes on financial management and investment. But some women simply draw strength from themselves. Alice Crouch expresses the perspective of those who want nothing to do with self-help groups. "I can't imagine anything worse," she declares, "than a group of women sitting around commiserating about what a terrible time they are having. I can't listen to myself talk, let alone listen to someone else's tale of woe. Support groups are all right, I suppose, for some women. But not for me." Alice was a successful community volunteer during her married life but never worked for pay. During her divorce, she was at square one financially but supported her teenage daughter and herself with part-time employment. She explains her point of view: "I don't like to be beaten down. I want people to be happy to see me and not say, 'Oh, here comes poor Alice.' I just take out my pride and dust it off. No one gets extra points for suffering in this life. Everybody suffers in some way."

Alice's attitude toward support groups is uncommon,

but divorced women who move on with their lives do warn that "workshop therapy" can become addictive. Women can make a cottage industry out of attending lectures, seminars, and workshops dealing with topics of divorce. If a woman stays dependent on these services, she delays the moment of risk taking that is necessary if she is to put the past behind her. Divorced women who shape their futures by making choices encourage others to be frank with themselves, admitting when they are using support services as a device to postpone making decisions about their lives. Unless a woman begins to act on the messages she is receiving from various types of professional assistance, her participation becomes a self-deluding exercise used to pass the time and perpetuate her role as a long-suffering ex-wife.

Divorced women who want to go on with new lives share their insecurities with only a few chosen confidantes whom they can count upon for comfort. Furthermore they look composed to the rest of the world because an attractive appearance makes them feel better about themselves. "If you are going through hell, you don't have to look like it," advises a young woman who dismantled a bedroom decorated for the arrival of an adopted infant when her husband admitted he was the father of a co-worker's newborn child.

"An attractive appearance will help you to project the message that you feel good about yourself, that you value yourself and that others should, too," offers a politician who looks ten years younger than her actual age of fifty-eight. But the former wife of a U.S. congressman clarifies that health care, diet, exercise, and a cosmetic makeover are all part of a woman's nurturing of herself. "After years of giving to a family, most women have to learn to take care of themselves," she says. "But if you want to establish a new life, then you don't want to look like something you no longer are, namely a wife." Her first practical suggestion is to "get a new hairdresser who will perceive you differently because you probably had a certain look as a 'nice wife.' Your first reaction will be, 'I've never worn my hair that way.' And that's right; you haven't." Cosmetics are more than cosmetic if they help a divorced woman to communicate who she is and how she feels, or wants to feel, about herself.

Beyond their best interests, divorced women can also continue to act like wives. An executive vice-president of a business firm, who rose from the ranks of volunteerism after her own divorce, always makes it a point to have lunch with newly separated women whom she knows. She recommends that they discontinue thinking of themselves as part-time employees or volunteers if their children are in school and their time is more flexible. "Women sometimes stay on one track, hiding out in middle-school libraries and museums three times a week. That's fine if that is really what a woman wants to do, but sometimes she is simply using these places as shelters. I always advise a divorced woman to find a job in the center of the city, where the action is. And to stop acting as if she is curtailed by a thousand family obligations if, in reality, that's not so."

A certificate of divorce can free a woman from marriage, but it does not provide her with the confidence and the will to free herself to seek personal fulfillment and separate from the role of wife. Furthermore, divorce initiates her into a cycle of conflicting emotions where she simultaneously savors peace and mourns lost dreams. But a divorced woman who is truly motivated to succeed can find many informal and formal support systems to help her endure and triumph over this period of transition. Women who do assert and affirm themselves after divorce insist that self-knowledge, however acquired, is the source that generates such transformation.

CHAPTER 8

Final Thoughts

Life can only be understood backwards; but it must
be lived forwards.

Sören Kierkegaard

A thirty-nine-year-old corporate attorney, the
mother of two young children, describes herself as being
in transition after fourteen years of marriage to a lawyer
in private practice. Until they had to alter their professional schedules after the birth of their children, Kitty
and Ray Harty were happily married. Tensions erupted
when Ray perceived that child care was mainly Kitty's
responsibility and congratulated himself for any help
he offered her. Kitty arranged an appointment with a
counselor when Ray finally remarked, "It's too bad that
you have to work. You are never here." Kitty admits
that she should have seen a counselor when the children
were babies but was embarrassed to do so. Ray joined
her in counseling, but criticism made him angry. Furthermore, when Kitty responded positively and tried to
change her behavior, Ray accused her of "faking."
They separated because Ray never understood Kitty's
insistence that child care was also his responsibility;
Kitty never understood Ray's need to have so much

time for himself. She saw him become a stern disciplinarian with the children because life had to be orderly if he were to count on having space for his own interests.

Divorced only a few months, Kitty claims that her marriage is behind her, but that it did not inevitably have to end. Trying to preserve harmony between her and Ray, Kitty pretended to ignore incubating tensions that should have been addressed. "Too many games go on with working couples about who does more. Who gets up with a sick child. Who attends soccer games. We play tricks with our office schedules, saying that we are expected at work, instead of confronting the issue with our spouses—that the problem of time is a serious one that we really need to solve together." But Kitty refuses to dwell on what might have been had she and Ray made a stronger effort to confront and communicate their problems at an early stage.

"Our marriage is over, and I must go on. I'm going to try to make Ray live up to his obligations with the children, but I can't absorb myself in carrying on a battle. I don't want to be obsessed with thinking and saying, 'You failed me.' I can't spend the rest of my life trying to think of ways to make him pay for what he did. I really want to get on to the forgiveness stage, but that's going to take a while. Right now I am concerned with raising the children by myself and establishing a new routine and life-style. If I concentrate only on how Ray has wronged me and the children, then I won't accomplish anything."

Long before she ever imagined that divorce would be in her future, Kitty wondered at the lost potential of a divorced woman in her neighborhood, a high school math teacher who focused her energies on trying to increase her husband's financial support. "She never took any risks with her own life, but she spent a fortune on legal proceedings trying to change the terms of her settlement. I always used to think, What a waste of time and money. She bored everyone because that was the only thing she ever talked about. You couldn't get around her anger to hear what she was really saying. I guess there are all kinds of role models."

Kitty does not speak this way just because she happens to be salaried as a corporate attorney. Having a professional career does not prevent a woman from fulfilling the stereotype of the passive, dependent female who must work at building self-confidence. For example, Kitty has to establish credit, as she had allowed her own credit to lapse. As a married woman she had no credit history because Ray handled all their bills and the mortgage and insurance payments. And she was happy to have him do so. But now she worries about her ability to manage a household budget and simultaneously create a happy home for her children while advancing in her career. She is haunted by domestic values that she knows are impossible to maintain: "I can rationalize that it is not important if I don't vacuum weekly, but I get a tight knot in my chest when I think about it." Working women, who know better, induce stress and damage their self-worth by wanting their homes to run as smoothly as when their own mothers stayed at home. But divorced women who have not completed college degrees often see higher education as their panacea, their answer to solving such tensions, building an independent life, and guaranteeing self-esteem.

College-educated women who divorce do have advantages. They trust their flexibility to call upon their skills to earn a living, even if they have not sustained a professional career during marriage. But acquiring self-esteem is more elusive than accumulating credits for a bachelor's degree or even pursuing a professional degree or earning a doctorate.

"Nothing is as destructive as low self-esteem," comments a tenured history professor at an Ivy League college. Married twenty-five years to a university English professor, Amanda Nelson assumed all the household obligations and child care responsibilities so that Jay could be free to live a life of the mind. No matter that her career was the equal of his in every way: superb teaching evaluations, essays published in prestigious academic journals, elected positions on important academic committees, and fellowships to teach abroad. Never receiving praise or the slightest compliment from Jay, Amanda kept trying to please and be perfect until "I prostrated myself on the altar of exhaustion and was on the brink of a nervous breakdown. I kept myself up to the maximum. If I were dressed for a cocktail party, he would say, 'You're not going to wear those shoes, are you?' If I published an article that received accolades from my colleagues, he would comment only on its weak points. I came to expect that he would diminish anything that I would do, no matter how important or inconsequential. I came to believe that I deserved such treatment. That laceration was somehow good for my soul," she says with an ironic laugh.

After her divorce, Amanda realized that she had been programmed to marry Jay because he responded to her accomplishments in the same manner as her parents did. Even though she was valedictorian of her high school class, her parents did not decide to attend the graduation ceremony until the last minute. That night when she was announced as the recipient of a full scholarship to a southern women's college, her parents never congratulated her. Amanda's accomplishments were not celebrated by her family, even when she was elected to Phi Beta Kappa. "Jay treated me in the only way that I ever knew. He reinforced my sense of inadequacy and the feelings I had about not really being very good."

Now that Amanda has married a man who thinks that she is intelligent and beautiful, she finds herself resisting his adulation. "I keep picking at the notion that someone I respect could think that I'm worth prizing. If you don't learn that you are special as a child, I don't think that you are ever convinced."

Education and economic security are neither a measure of a woman's self-worth nor a guarantee that she will attain it. But one learns from the case of Amanda Nelson and others like her that self-knowledge is necessary for the development of self-esteem. By probing her past, Amanda understands its influence on the choices she has made in her life. She did not repeat the mistake of marrying a man whose demeaning attitude toward her would, paradoxically, make her feel comfortable, although unhappy. She no longer lives with the certainty of knowing that she will have to respond to belittling comments. Rather, she risks vulnerability in learning how to react to praise. Facing how she felt about herself as a child and teenager because of the way her parents treated her, Amanda is able to understand and modify her present behavior to serve her own best interests.

Unlike Amanda Nelson, a seventy-two-year-old woman, divorced for over twenty years, enjoys sweet memories of her parents. She picks through them, attributing her successes as an actress, politician, and antique dealer to the fact that she remains her father's daughter. She delights in confiding that as a teenager she overheard her father remark to her mother, "When Fran was four years old, she had more personality than Eleanor Roosevelt!"

The daughter of a country physician, Fran Meade still remembers how her father made house calls throughout the Kentucky countryside, treating patients of every income. "My father was not a churchgoing man, but he was deeply spiritual. He didn't know what it meant to be bigoted or self-righteous. He loved people and ideas, and always had discussions with me. He taught all the time, and encouraged me to read anything I could get my hands on. When I was very young, I remember talking and talking with my parents at the dinner table. They really seemed to enjoy my sense of humor and what I had to say."

Fran graduated from high school at the height of the Depression and notes that the deepest regret of her life was that she was not able to go on to college. But she did begin writing for a local newspaper, covering "fires, births, and weddings at ten cents an inch. After growing up in a household that encouraged free expression, working on a newspaper seemed perfectly natural to me." At age nineteen she married a twenty-six-year-old pharmacist, "and we worked together to make ends meet. But he returned from the war without any initiative. He had been used to taking orders, while during the war years, I developed even more independence."

The balance tipped in Fran Meade's life when she and her husband bought a house on the edge of a midwestern college campus. Soon Fran's home became a "Left Bank salon" for professors and students who gathered on Thursday nights after classes to drink coffee and enjoy freshly baked bread. "I was educated then. . . ." Fran pauses. "I adored my father, but I always resented the fact that he was not able to provide for my college education." The more Fran and her academic friends discussed religion, race, agriculture, politics, and sex, the more Hank Meade retired to enjoy his own company. Inspired by political conversation, Fran joined the Young Republicans at age thirty-eight and the next year was elected president of her region and delegate to the national convention of 1956. Responding to the comment that her picture with Richard Nixon, hanging over her cookbooks in the kitchen on the wall beside the parrot's cage, is a cut above the obligatory pose because they actually seem to be talking, Fran replies, "Oh, I'm generally able to engage someone, no matter who it is."

As Fran's visibility in the community increased, Hank

remained in the shadows, disgruntled by his wife's popularity. From politics she turned to the stage. Never having acted before, she auditioned for a summer stock production of *Bell, Book and Candle* and won the lead role. Over the next few years she had major parts in nine more plays, ending with *Blithe Spirit*. And although Hank grew more sullen, the couple made no effort to divorce.

But more significant than her roles in politics or the theater was the career Fran Meade developed as a leading antique dealer in the Potomac-Virginia area. "I was born knowing antiques," she claims, "because I had read so many novels where the characters enjoyed Tiffany silver or Wedgwood china or Turkish carpets. When I saw my first Turkish carpet, I felt very much at home because my mind had always been furnished with these things."

In the early years of her marriage, Fran bought "old things" to furnish her house elegantly but inexpensively. Her antique business began serendipitously when other women admired her objects and offered to buy them. But as Fran became successful, Hank grew more distant from his family. Yet she made no effort to divorce until she was financially able to support three children through high school and college. When she knew that her business would be lucrative, she startled the present but absent Hank by telling him that she wanted a divorce.

Fran Meade claims that she was open to creative challenges because of her father's influence: "I'll always remember his saying, 'On Judgment Day you will be asked to explain why you didn't enjoy those things which God put here to be enjoyed.' That was his inspiring philosophy, and it still nurtures me. But my husband was just the opposite. I think women have to realize that there are a lot worse things than being lonely. If you are in a bad marriage, being lonely can be a luxury compared with being married to someone you shouldn't be."

Fran Meade's wisdom did not come too late. She always knew that the man she married was not the one for whom her father's joie de vivre had prepared her to spend her life. But economic pragmatism and social pressure influenced even him to persuade his daughter to a "good match." He was sufficiently conditioned to bless her marriage to a traditionalist whom she would soon outgrow.

Looking a spry fifty-five, Fran Meade approaches her seventy-second birthday with bittersweet observations: "I am psychologically free and so secure that right now I feel that I could accomplish anything I set my mind to do. But age and health won't permit it. I guess I'm a late bloomer. In one way I lived a very sheltered life as a child, learning how to sew and cook, but my father helped me to discover the world of conversation and ideas. Talk . . . I guess that's still what I do best and when I'm happiest. Talking and learning. I've been a successful antique dealer because I love to learn about things. And that goes way back, to my father. I wasn't out of a pattern, and I never will be."

For Fran, the purpose of remembering is to reflect on the positive influence her father continues to have on her. The bond between Fran and her father, as well as that between Amanda Nelson and her father, remains important to these women and their self-identity. Their consciousness of the dynamics of these relationships is crucial to their understanding of their marriages and, inevitably, of their own needs. Neither woman can rewrite her past and chalk in different choices. But when a woman awakens to the personal and societal restraints in her life, she frees herself for the future, even at age seventy-two.

After her divorce, a woman who basked in happiness confides that she also was held to her past. She constantly had medical appointments to check out stomach problems, headaches, and suspected tumors. Having spent over twenty years finely tuned to her husband's every need, she seldom noticed her own aches and pains. Now free to concentrate on herself, she lacked judgment about her mildest ailment. But more important, she realized that she was manufacturing her symptoms: "I simply did not know how to deal with feeling good, and became a hypochondriac. I was indulging a fatalistic attitude for no purpose. I created physical symptoms as a deliberate threat, because I could not believe my good fortune. I didn't think my happiness could possibly be sustained."

Whether self-awareness is acquired through psychoanalysis, private or group therapy, quiet introspection, or reading, self-knowledge is indispensable for a divorced woman who truly wants to escape the traps of the past and begin a life that is worthy of her.

Women who are successful in professional careers are

often reluctant to accept therapy as necessary for themselves during divorce. Although they know better than to do so, they attach a stigma to psychological treatment when it comes to their own psyche. Like men who have preceded them in the corporate structure, their private needs become submerged in a public role. They feel weak and inadequate if unable to deal with personal problems when their days are spent analyzing complex legal or economic issues. Furthermore, despite the sexual revolution and divorce rate, the myth dies hard that a woman is a personal failure if her marriage does not succeed. The old formula for marriage—where husbands and wives have distinct roles—has changed, but the compromises and tensions are not clear cut on a day-to-day basis when couples are faced with problems and choices. It has long been a part of marital advice that husbands should be breadwinners and protectors, whereas wives are comforters who do not compete. The answer for all marriages is not the same, but this generation is at the cutting edge of balancing love, children, marriage, and work. Thus divorced wives who have maintained careers may be secure financially regarding their futures, but they are often afloat in admitting, seeking, and finding the emotional support necessary for defining their personal lives. Moreover, family and friends can be slow to offer consolation because "she's so competent that certainly she can deal with this upset in her life."

A divorced stockbroker received little comfort from her family until therapy helped her to say to them, "Hey, I'm frightened, just as you would be. I may handle stocks and bonds well, but I'm having a terrible time with my divorce."

When a professional woman divorces she probably recognizes her needs well enough to know that she has to choose a therapist who does not suffer from a post-Freudian hangover. But weary from domestic conflict and absorbed in creating a peaceful home for her children, she may not invest enough energy in looking for a compatible therapist. Women who do not have easy access to an urban area especially have limited options for psychological therapy.

One divorced mother with two young children, who is a landscape architect living in a bucolic area seventy miles from the largest city, practiced her art between the children's school day, music lessons, and soccer games. Short of time, she chose to see a semiretired psychiatrist in the neighboring community as her therapist. Out of convenience she stayed with him for months before acknowledging that he was not helping her to rewrite the role she felt preordained to play as "ideal woman." Instead he actually encouraged her to become the perfect teacher, nurse, bookkeeper, spiritual director, seamstress, housekeeper, cook, and chauffeur, a message she absorbed by trying to juggle an insane schedule. Finally she saw the light, restructured her time, arranged for the children to have good care, and drove the seventy miles each week to see a psychiatrist who was highly recommended by trusted friends.

Some women choose to undergo therapy with a woman because they think they will relate to her more easily, particularly if they fear transferring their anger toward their husbands to a male psychiatrist or psychologist. As with the lawyers whom they retain, women prefer therapists who are free of patriarchial attitudes and theory, whether or not they are male or female.

Although women going through divorce want to be understood and often form new friendships with other divorced women, one of them points out that the camaraderie born of divorce is often artificial and provokes stress. Admitting that her style is to face her problems quietly, Elsie Schoyer was inundated with calls from friends and acquaintances when word got out that she and her husband had separated. Women she hardly knew invited her for lunch or dinner to offer advice. "Some women really intrude under the guise of establishing a network, when they really have a need to rehash their own war story. I simply recoiled because what works for one doesn't work for another. Each story is different, and the common bond can only be that we care about each other. But some women are rabid that you solve your problems their way."

Elsie clarifies her point by drawing the analogy of lending a book: "When someone gives you a book to read, you feel compelled to read it immediately so that the next time you can say, 'Yes, I read it.' But all the time you're reading, you also are thinking, Why did she give me this? What am I supposed to see? What message am I supposed to get? Extraordinary strings are attached to giving a book! Extraordinary strings are also attached when a casual acquaintance who is divorced insists that you need to suffer her wisdom. Divorced women can presume too much of each other, and I absolutely resent unsolicited intrusion."

Women can intrude on each other's privacy by presuming that divorce is a common denominator binding them together. Sometimes women have to question their lives by themselves and, as they change, lose certain friends in the process. "I always have in the back of my mind, 'Beware the best friend,'" confides a divorce attorney who knows the strings that often are attached to a client. Finally exasperated with a client who kept complaining that she was receiving only seven hundred dollars monthly for child support as contrasted with her neighbor, also with one child, who was receiving twelve hundred, the attorney snapped, "Maybe your friend's husband is richer than yours. Maybe you should have married him."

On the other hand, women who do not weigh the advice of others, and simply forge ahead by themselves into the complex territory of divorce, can make serious mistakes. If they are too eager to cut the cord with the past, they can particularly sabotage their financial futures by refusing to spend time in litigation. Women frequently confess to having stopped the efforts of lawyers to negotiate financial settlements that were, indeed, more just. In retrospect, some women regret their easy appeasement. Others, although strapped financially, still say that economic security was not worth the cost of what they perceived as continued dissension.

When a woman capitulates to a facile financial settlement, refusing to press for what is due her, one is tempted to wish she would "think more like a man," even though the expression no longer carries the weight of an automatic compliment. In her study, *In a Different Voice*, Carol Gilligan points out the differences in the way men and women think and the values that they hold. Just because women are oriented toward caring about people, maintaining relationships, and avoiding violent solutions to problems does not mean that they should exclude themselves from the group of people whose quality of life concerns them. In the long run a woman who refrains from asserting herself at the time of her divorce settlement because she craves the respite of peace may very well be hurting herself and those closest to her by limiting her future economic security. A divorced woman can even elevate herself to public martyrdom by showing how she was cheated. But the truth may be that under the guise of not wanting to sustain conflict, she chose to be a passive victim, counter to her lawyer's best advice.

Opposite advice may seem to be offered by a corporate vice-president, divorced for eight years: "The best thing a divorced woman can do for herself is to get off the dole and stop wasting energy thinking about the better settlement she thinks she should have had. She needs to get out and work." When a woman paralyzes her life trying to squeeze more money out of her ex-husband, she is victimizing herself just as much as the wife who settles for far less than her share. Her identity becomes absorbed in making sure that the world knows that her husband will not get away with having caused her humiliation and pain. In wanting more than a divorce decree to prove that her suffering is genuine, a woman limits her self-actualization and becomes her own enemy.

Again, during divorce proceedings a woman should expect to be fully informed and knowledgeable about her financial condition. Then she must be frank with herself in understanding her motivations for choosing to accept or reject the terms of settlement advised by her attorney. She can cultivate a role as victimized woman by agreeing to a lesser financial arrangement as well as by pursuing an unrealistic one: in either case, she is continuing to define herself in relation to her ex-husband.

The women interviewed for this book concur that it is difficult for divorced women to adjust to living in a society where couples reign. A divorced man by himself can be reduced to being a welcome commodity at cocktail parties, but a divorced woman is often perceived as having eyes on her best friend's husband. Shortly after her separation, a woman who later began a successful kitchenware business was immediately excluded from monthly gourmet dinners that she and her husband had enjoyed together with a group of married couples. "I really found out who my true friends were, and was so sad that married friends stopped asking me to do things. But through my business I eventually began meeting new people and had a much broader experience. Now, it's nice to see my old friends, but I really feel I've grown beyond them and can't imagine returning to a more insular life."

But the issue of social identity is larger than losing

invitations to private dinner parties. Once a woman truly changes the orientation of her thinking and confronts a life alone, she begins to value herself as a whole person, not as half of a person freakishly amputated by divorce. She becomes less concerned with the validity of the roles she used to play and grows more focused on finding her real self that exists underneath all of them. She uncovers the strengths, skills, and social preferences that make her a unique individual. A divorced woman has two options: to allow others to influence the way she feels about herself or to discover what she wants and work to make her dreams come true. Concentrating her creative energy on herself, a divorced woman will experience the freedom of her own evolution, thus causing her to lose friends of the past while discovering others.

To avoid this uncomfortable process of self-evaluation, a divorced woman may remarry too soon in order to stop feeling incomplete without a husband. But the women interviewed for this book maintain that to remarry is not the way to bypass the loneliness of divorce, however tempting. They would agree with the woman who said at the end of her marriage, "This is not the script I would have chosen to write for myself." But they also agree that a woman best spends her time after divorce learning who she is and who she can become. Living through the chaos of a disintegrating marriage and then the emotional devastation of divorce, few women emerge without violated self-esteem. Academic achievement and financial security do not insulate a wife from interiorizing her husband's value of her. Only when she is secure in the knowledge of her personal strengths and needs can a divorced woman enter into marriage reasonably sure that she will not gamble away her identity for a second time. "Wimpy men marry wimpy women; secure men marry independent women," offers a divorced Cape Cod land developer who respects herself and her achievements too much to settle for a "wimpy man."

Another woman, who lived a country club existence until after her divorce, borrowed small amounts of money to start a successful catering business. "When I was married, I always thought I was independent, but I really wasn't. My husband never objected to anything I wanted to do because he really didn't care that much about me. One morning when I was taking a shower, he poked his head inside the door and said, 'I'm leaving.' Like a fool, I answered, 'Where are you going?' He said, 'I don't know yet.' And that was the end of eighteen years of marriage. It was the most devastating experience of my life, but now I'm thankful for it. Otherwise I would be sitting around the country club pool, without any idea of what I am able to accomplish. But now that I've developed my own business, I am independent enough to know that it would have to be a 'great someone' for me to risk remarrying. I would never go back to where I was."

But one cannot pretend that the forty-five women represented in *Divorced Women, New Lives* do not continue to round sharp corners. "I'm not Rocky at the top of the stairs," says one with a self-deprecating laugh. Yet, like the others, she continues to grow in confidence, achieving here and there a degree of self-fulfillment that seemed impossible in the aftermath of divorce. One year after their interviews, the women continue to make important choices.

Phyllis Corbett, who attempted suicide seven years ago, moved from Manhattan to accept a position as executive vice-president of a major New England software firm. Jessica Schumann now writes essays, poetry, and fiction for national publications. Isabel Howell has had successful exhibitions of her art, selling her canvases for anywhere between five and six thousand dollars. Sandy Jeffries faced a diagnosis of low-grade depression, now remedied by medication. Still trying to direct her future, she has left real estate to begin a graduate program in career counseling. Barbara Reed has married. Other women are close to marrying men who will take pride in their accomplishments. Alice Crouch graduated from a part-time position in cosmetic sales to become the chief South Atlantic representative for a glitzy perfume manufacturer, more than tripling the salary of her first job. She fooled friends on her forty-second birthday by inviting them to her own surprise party.

Although the women interviewed would never return to their previous lives, each of them knows what it means to be scared about her future. After divorce they were able to move forward only by learning to trust themselves to size up their personal situations and then to act. They know the slow rhythm of picking up the pieces. Divorce often drives women who cultivate such self-reliance into an interior privacy, where they score their own milestones quietly. Yet rituals, even ones like drinking coffee while taping an interview, can provide a miracle of momentary insight where one wonders at the fact that life can be redeemed. For it is not accidental change that marks the character of these women's lives, but deep personal renewal. Indeed, a sense of responsibility about helping others motivated all of the women to tell their stories. Willingly they reflected on their pasts as a way of connecting with the troubled lives of unseen women who have yet to bring their own choices into the light of consciousness.

Eulogy

The question I am most asked about this book is whether or not I was depressed by hearing so many stories of personal tragedy. The answer, surprisingly, is no. The women I interviewed confided their intimate experiences of emotional starvation, psychological turmoil, and physical abuse. Yet their pride in their accomplishments rescued me from dwelling on their suffering. Each woman's determination to reverse the direction of her life renewed my understanding that time is pure potentiality. Indeed, as we talked they artfully deflected any self-pity. With a focus on the future, none of the women is hostage to her memories.

Few of them had ever measured, in fact, the distances that they had traveled since walking through the "burning door." Until understanding that my interview allowed them an opportunity to look back and appreciate themselves, I was surprised when women thanked me. On the telephone the next day, Nancy Stewart, who owns her own insurance company and is happily remarried, confided: "I never really stopped to think about how far I've come since those days when I couldn't even tell my parents about how terrible my marriage was because they would have said it was all my fault. The loneliness was devastating. Talking to you and remembering it all was therapeutic."

Her words jolted me. If therapeutic for her, then more so for me. For in her voice, I heard my mother's.

My mother was married at sixteen, divorced at eighteen, and remarried in her mid-twenties. But she never told me this until a week before my own wedding. Maybe the real reason I pursued these interviews and wrote this book was somehow to erase her embarrassment and find a way to understand her need to be silent. Maybe I want to forgive her for the hurt I still have that she had kept her secret from me for the first twenty-six years of my life, when the rest of the world knew. What kind of craziness was that?

My childhood was always uneasy. And now am I writing a book to make sense of why it had to be that way? Is this what divorced women mean when they say that without "bumping into trees," they would not be where they are now? Is this the final connection I have with women like Nancy Stewart, who so willingly revealed themselves when I asked my questions? Was I asking the questions that no one had asked my mother? Was I asking the questions that she never had answered for me? Was I proving that her answers would not have made me cringe, die, drive away mad, a lost daughter?

A week before my wedding, I parked my car at the side of the road so that Mother could tell me a halting story of the handsome young man who had arrived in town. A Catholic, she was married by a Lutheran minister on a date that I do not know. Early in their marriage, her boyish husband pushed her down the stairs.

172

He broke her nose. I do not know when or why he left her. I only know that he had a hazel eye. She told me that my sister was his child and not my father's daughter. Shaken, I held on to the family story of Daddy once buying her five little dresses, each one the same. It now made poignant sense. He was learning to be a father.

Muriel Rukeyser is right: the world does "split open" when one woman tells her story. I wanted to pull up trees and hurl them at the sky. I hurt for my mother's life, but I was also angry that she had never entrusted it to me.

I had always sensed that something I could not name was not the way it should have been in my family. I had attended a Catholic, all-girls private school, but my parents seldom went to church. Until the week of my wedding, I could never ask why. Now I trembled with knowing the banality of tragedy in the lives of everyday people.

Growing up, I preferred my father's world of action to the troubled waters that surrounded my mother's. I became shy when my intrusion caused her conversations with friends or my sister to change direction. I felt more embraced, more comfortable, at Forbes Field watching baseball games with Daddy, yelling at Pirates manager Bill Meyer to take out the starting pitcher: "Put a fork in him; he's done." My father was a sports promoter. Gus Lesnevich was light-heavyweight champion. Visiting New York City as a nine-year-old, I wanted to meet Nat Fleischer, the editor of *Ring Magazine*. In his office at Madison Square Garden, Mr. Fleischer shook my hand, squeaked around on a swivel chair, chomped on a cigar, and insisted that Tony Zale's six-round knockout of Rocky Graziano was the fight of the decade, maybe the century. Even I found the conversation to be interminable. But I was happy being close to the heartbeat of boxing while Mother went shopping at Lord & Taylor.

I was never too precious to snoop around the old Pittsburgh Lyceum where fighters trained. I was never too young to visit the smoke-filled offices of sports writers, where I kept one eye on the ticker-tape machine, pretending that I had a deadline to meet. Yet I was too fragile to grow up knowing my mother's story of marriage and divorce.

Now, ten years after her death, I catch images of her in the words women use with me to describe the pain of divorce. I ache for the woman who told me that she and another young mother exchanged only quiet signals about their unhappy marriages while playing with their children at a community swimming pool. "To be divorced even in 1971 was to be a pariah!" How must my mother have felt decades earlier? I have a fleeting memory of sitting on a beach with her in the late 1940s. When she lit a cigarette and turned to a friend, was she talking about that first marriage, which I was not to know about? How did she feel when she leaned against a sink, pregnant with my sister? What talisman did she hold in her hand to convince herself she had a future? Did she ever cry over an Easter basket and then buy candy for me? I try to harbor images of my mother as a young woman. But never feeling free to ponder what I never was allowed to talk about, I cannot sustain them.

I still do not know the story of Mother's first marriage. Yet so many other women have told me theirs. When one of them claims that her interview with me made her feel "whole," I am redeemed. For in her voice I hear my mother's, and, at last, I feel blessed. By listening to women, now years younger than she, I hear the truth of my mother's silence. She craved not the absolution of a priest in the confessional, but belief in her own good spirit. She needed only to release her words, so that her life could be received and celebrated. If a woman tells her own story with trust, the earth will not crack open. It will heal, deeply, from inside. Trust nurtures love and understanding across tables and tape recorders, across graves, bonding ghosts of the past that help us to create. A woman does not betray herself or shatter others by revealing her heart's need. How could my mother have gained that wisdom? The time was not ripe for either of us.

ABOUT THE AUTHOR

ELLIE WYMARD taught some of the first courses on women offered in the country at Carlow College, where she is Professor of English and Chair of the Division of Humanities. Her doctorate is from the University of Pittsburgh. Her critical essays on writers have appeared in scholarly journals. She lives in Pittsburgh, Pennsylvania, and Chatham, Massachusetts, with her husband, an attorney, and their two sons.